Conspicuous Compassion

Conspicuous Compassion: why sometimes it really is cruel to be kind

Patrick West

Civitas: Institute for the Study of Civil Society
London

First published February 2004

© The Institute for the Study of Civil Society 2004
The Mezzanine, Elizabeth House
39 York Road, London SE1 7NQ
email: books@civitas.org.uk

ISBN 1-903 386-34 9

Typeset by Civitas
in New Century Schoolbook

Printed in Great Britain by
The Cromwell Press
Trowbridge, Wiltshire

Contents

Author

Patrick West is a freelance writer. Born in London in 1974, he graduated from Manchester University in 1997 with an MA in cultural history. He has written for *The Times*, the *Daily Telegraph*, the *Irish Times*, the *New Statesman*, the *Spectator*, the *Times Literary Supplement*, *Prospect*, the *Irish Post*, the *Sunday Independent* (Ireland), the *Catholic Herald* and *Living Marxism* (*LM*). He writes a weekly column for *spiked-online.com*.

Acknowledgments

Special thanks to Peter Hitchens, Ruth Hornsby, Mick Hume, Brendan O'Neill, Jemima Miéville, Edward West and Robert Whelan for helping this book to happen, and to my parents, Richard and Mary, for their support and inspiration.

Patrick West
London and Dublin, December 2003

Foreword

Thomas Hobbes, back in the seventeenth century, based his political philosophy on the belief that one of the greatest of human pleasures—perhaps the greatest—was feeling superior to others. It was so powerful a drive that those who lacked any real superiority would resort to fantasy—what he called 'vainglory'. A century ago, the radical American sociologist Thorstein Veblen elaborated this view as a sociology of the rich. In *The Theory of the Leisure Class*, he documented in great detail how the powerful would demonstrate their superiority—in ways ranging from Chinese mandarins whose absurdly long fingernails demonstrated how far they were above vulgar things, to educated Europeans expressing themselves in Latin tags to show off their education. He called this form of conduct 'conspicuous consumption'. Veblen was a utilitarian. He thought that a lot of what we call culture was just showing off.

Patrick West is not a utilitarian, but has made a brilliant use of Veblen's critical machinery to expose one of the dominant assumptions of our age: namely, that to exhibit feelings about public events and public figures demonstrates superiority of soul. His book is a catalogue of the ingenious devices we have developed to make this clear to others. He does not shirk the element of menace sometimes added to the mix, menace directed against those who might think their feelings to be their own business. We want such mavericks to think and feel the way we do. They too must wear their hearts on their lapels. We pretend to feel the pain of others, and signal it by sentimentalising beggars, moments (lengthening rapidly into minutes and minutes) of silence, by apologising for things we never did, by signing petitions, and a variety of other gestures.

The cynics of the seventeenth century were acutely aware of the vice of hypocrisy, which La Rochefoucauld described as the tribute vice pays to virtue. But the hypocrite usually knew perfectly well that he was pretending. His dishonesty was for the outside world, not usually for his inner life. The alarming thing about our own conspicuous compassion is that its bearers seem to believe in their own emotions—though (as West makes clear) they don't actually believe in their feelings to the point where they lose control of their wallets. Conspicuous compassion, as a simple matter of fact, often correlates with decreasing contributions to charity. The decline of fortitude as a British virtue in the face of new technologies such as counselling and stress management is a well-documented feature of our times, but West's theme is the way in which we actually disapprove of fortitude even in others.

Feelings and thoughts are part of the inner life, but when so much is externalised in gestures, one can only wonder how much of inner life remains. Traditional religious spirituality has long been declining, but amidst the politicised righteousness of the contemporary world, what is left, we may wonder, of integrity, honesty and real concern for others?

West quotes Oscar Wilde's remark that a sentimentalist is someone who wants the pleasure of an emotion without paying the price for it. It's not often that Wilde was profound, but here he cut to the essence of moral gesturing.

West is the Seurat of social critics. He is a *pointilliste* who has created a canvas out of particulars: the strange emotions on display in the public realm. It is in confronting the details *en masse*, details we encounter drip by drip in everyday life, that we may begin to understand what they tell us about our civilisation.

Kenneth Minogue

1

Conspicuous Compassion

*'Observe how children weep and cry, so that they will be pitied
... the thirst for pity is a thirst for self-enjoyment, and at the
expense of one's fellow men'*
                                        Friedrich Nietzsche
                                'Human, All Too Human', 1878

WE live in an age of conspicuous compassion. Immodest alms-giving may be as old as humanity—consider the tale of Jesus rebuking the self-exalting Pharisee—but it has flowered spectacularly of recent. We are given to ostentatious displays of empathy to a degree hitherto unknown. We sport countless empathy ribbons, send flowers to recently deceased celebrities, weep in public over the deaths of murdered children, apologise for historical misdemeanours, wear red noses for the starving of Africa, go on demonstrations to proclaim 'Drop the Debt' or 'Not in My Name'. We feel each other's pain. In the West in general and Britain in particular, we project ourselves as humane, sensitive and sympathetic souls. Today's three Cs are not, as one minister of education said, 'culture, creativity and community', but rather, as commentator Theodore Dalrymple has put it, 'compassion, caring and crying in public'.[1]

This book's thesis is that such displays of empathy do not change the world for the better: they do not help the poor, diseased, dispossessed or bereaved. Our culture of ostentatious caring concerns, rather, projecting one's ego, and informing others what a deeply caring individual you are. It is about feeling good, not doing good, and illustrates not how altruistic we have become, but how selfish.

Consider the growth of looped empathy ribbons. Since their appearance in the 1990s, donations to charities have

1

not actually grown. Far from 'raising awareness', ribbons serve merely to inform one's peers how terribly concerned one is about Aids, cancer sufferers or children with leukaemia. We live in a generation that is fond of signing web petitions to 'stop war'—petitions that do nothing of the sort. It has manifested itself in that slogan 'Not In My Name', a phrase that suggests that today's 'anti-war' protesters are no longer concerned with stopping conflict, but merely announcing their personal disapproval of it. 'Drop the Debt' say others, forming human chains around G8 meetings, shoving in our faces photographs of emaciated Ethiopians.

This phenomenon is not some harmless foible. Outlandish and cynical displays of empathy can bring about decidedly 'uncaring' consequences. In terms of the Third World, 'dropping the debt' may not help starving Africans at all. It may make their lives worse by rewarding their kleptocratic governments, freeing up their budgets to buy more guns to perpetuate their pointless wars. We like to be spotted giving alms to beggars, yet such an action can have the contrary result. Most beggars spend their alms on alcohol or hard drugs. Giving him your spare change is not a humane act, it may keep him on the street.

Why do we so desperately want to show that we love and care for strangers? According to the philosopher Stjepan Mesotrovic, it is because we live in a post-emotional age, one characterised by crocodile tears and manufactured emotion. This, he posits, is a symptom of post-modernity. In a shallow age in which reality and fiction have blurred, in which we are constantly bombarded with news bulletins, soap operas and 'reality television', our capacity to feel authentic, deep emotions has withered. In this cynical state, he posits, we no longer want to change the world; we want merely to 'be nice'.[2] This is indeed part of the problem, though I believe that conspicuous compassion, more accurately, is a symptom of what the psychologist Oliver James has dubbed our 'low serotonin' society. We are given to such displays of empathy because we want to be loved ourselves. Despite being healthier, richer and better-off than in living memory, we are not happier. Rather, we are more depressed than ever. This is because we have become atomised and lonely. Binding institutions such as the Church, marriage, the family and the nation have withered in the post-war era. We have turned into communities of strangers. Raised in fragmented family units, more and more of us live by ourselves. According to the Office for National Statistics, the percentage of Britons living by themselves in 1971 was 18 per cent; by 2002 it was 29 per cent. Fifty-four per cent do not know their neighbours; 27 per cent say they have no close friends living nearby.[3] Television and the impossible promises of consumerism have cruelly raised expectations of how happy and successful we *should* be. We are led to believe that buying more products will make our lives complete, and we too will be as content as the women on that advert. We view television as a mirror of reality, and thereby become disheartened that our existence is not as funny as that enjoyed by the protagonists in *Friends*, as cosy and friendly as those in *Cheers* or as socially intimate as by those in *Coronation Street*.[4]

As a consequence, depression levels have rocketed in the post-war era.[5] 'The collapse of marriage and of the close social networks that characterised our ancestors is a major cause of low-serotonin problems: depression, aggression, compulsions', concludes James in his 1998 work *Britain on the Couch*, 'We are supposed to have become a society of Woody Allens, obsessing about trivia and unanswerable philosophical dilemmas to fill the void left by war and plague'.[6] According to the Future Foundation, the proportion of people suffering from 'anxiety, depression or bad nerves' has risen from just over five per cent to just under nine per cent in the last ten years. It cites as a reason increased atomisation and the decline in deference for institutions such as the Church, which leave more people with fewer places to seek refuge in times of trial.[7] The State has made divorce far easier, yet divorcees are much more likely to suffer almost every low-serotonin problem than people in intact relationships.[8] The welfare state has helped us become a nation of loners, of single-parents, divorcees, fatherless children. In this regard, James notes:

Divorce, gender rancour and the isolation of children from depressed or absent parents have all increased since 1950 and
between them, play a large role in increasing the numbers of low-
serotonin people'.[9]

No wonder we are given to crying in public. And no
wonder we seek to do so collectively. Ostentatious caring
allows a lonely nation to forge new social bonds. Addition-
ally, it serves as a form of catharsis. Its most visible manifestation is the habit of coming together to cry over the
death of celebrities or murdered children. We saw this at its
most ghoulish after the demise of Diana, Princess of Wales.
In truth, the mourners were not crying for her, but for
themselves. These deaths serve as an opportunity to
(in)articulate our own unhappiness, and, by doing so in
public, to form new social ties to replace those that have
disappeared.

Such displays are sheer opportunism. They do not reflect,
as some contend, that Britain has thankfully cast off its
collective 'stiff upper lip'. They are the symptoms of a
cynical nation. To judge by the 'outpourings of grief' over
Diana in August 1997, one would have thought her memory
would have remained firmly imprinted on the public's
consciousness. Yet, on the fifth anniversary of her death in
August 2002, there were no crowds, tears or teddies. Diana
had served her purpose. The public had moved on. These
recreational grievers were now emoting about Jill Dando,
Linda McCartney or the Soham girls.

The phrase used to describe this phenomenon, 'conspicuous compassion', will for many readers seem merely a play
on Thorstein Veblen's more familiar phrase: 'conspicuous
consumption'. But the two phenomena share more than
linguistic similarity. Conspicuous consumption, as Veblen
wrote in 1912, is concerned with the leisure class manifest-
ing its position of power through extreme and often deliber-
ately wasteful displays of wealth. Thus, it too is concerned
with social one-up-manship. 'The consumption of luxuries,'
Veblen wrote, is 'a mark of the master', and '[s]ince the
consumption of these more excellent goods is evidence of
wealth, it becomes honorific; and conversely, the failure to
consume in due quantity and quality becomes a mark of

inferiority and demerit'.[10] Similarly, the failure to emote in due quantity and quality becomes a mark of inferiority in our society of conspicuous compassion.

To today's collective 'carers', the fate of the homeless, starving Africans or dead celebrities is not actually of principal importance. What really drives their behaviour is the need to be seen to care. And they want to be seen displaying compassion because they want to be loved themselves. Yet as we will see, sometimes it can be cruel to care.

2

Mourning Sickness

The death of Diana, Princess of Wales, on 31 August 1997, came as a shock to most people. It was a tragedy that a young woman was struck down so violently in the prime of her life. Yet the reaction to her death proved equally, if not more, alarming. In the wake of her death, thousands queued for up to eight hours to sign one of the 43 books of condolence. Thousands were seen on television bulletins elbowing their way into music stores to buy multiple copies of Elton John's lament for 'England's Rose' —*Candle in the Wind*—each trying to stack more copies in their arms than the next man. The mass mourning outside Kensington and Buckingham palaces, the flowers, the teddy bears, the crowds that lined her funeral route, Tony Blair's chin-wobbling tribute to the 'People's Princess'—never had Britain witnessed such a collective outpouring of emoting.

Some commentators applauded this transformation. They deemed it healthy that a nation renowned for its emotionally suffocating stiff-upper-lip apparently now felt comfortable in wearing its feelings on its collective sleeve. But to others it aroused the suspicion that this was mere ersatz emoting, a symptom of the infantalisation of Britain. The real question was: for whom were the mourners crying—the 'Queen of Hearts', or themselves?

We have become addicted to showy public displays of empathy because we are a lonely and unhappy society. We use the death of strangers, quite cynically, to forge social bonds to assert how caring we are, and to be 'one of the crowd'. The strangers come and go—the children of Dunblane, Princess Diana, the Soham girls—but the malady remains. This is because we suffer from chronic mourning sickness.

In 1987, a lone gunman in the Berkshire town of Hungerford massacred 16 people in a random act of violence. The nation may have been shocked then, yet there were no teddy bears, flowers, condolences books and weeping in public. Even the death of 95 Liverpool fans at the Hillsborough stadium in Sheffield in 1989 failed to generate mass displays of grieving throughout the country. There was grief and anger, yet this was relatively localised on Merseyside. The entire country did not stop for repeated minutes silence. Still, the mass display of flowers at Liverpool's Anfield stadium hinted that change was occurring.

By the early 1990s the flowers had begun to blossom. During his life Freddie Mercury was the singer in a rock group, Queen. In death he became an icon and a martyr. A concert at Wembley Stadium in 1991 was held in his honour, where his peers and fans came to display their sorrow. The murder of 16 children in Dunblane in March 1996 provoked an even more emotive response. Politicians of all parties visited the Scottish town to make known their condolences, and people from around the UK did likewise in the form of floral tributes and cards.

Some took heart from Britain's reaction to Dunblane and Diana. It illustrated that we were not a selfish nation, but a giving and caring one. 'I want to begin by saying how proud I was to be British on Saturday', said Tony Blair a week after Diana's funeral, 'when the whole world could see our country united in grief, compassion and a determination that her memory should be honoured and good made to come of the tragedy that was her death.'[1] Rabbi Jonathan Sacks argued that the reaction to the Dunblane killings had proved that Britain was 'not a nation of individuals living disconnected lives in pursuit of self-interest, but a people united by a sense of fellow feeling'. The Archbishop of Canterbury, George Carey, echoed the Chief Rabbi's words: 'We also know that compassion, love and solidarity and, in the aftermath of Dunblane, the faithful devotion of parents and teachers towards children in their care, are more than "nice". They are absolutely good. Let us build on these'.[2] But such sentiments begged the questions: what kind of society requires the horrific deaths of children to bond together? And how disrespectful and exploitative is it to do so? Rather than being a demonstration of how compassionate and communitarian the British were, such a reaction revealed how alienated and opportunistic we had become.

And intolerant too. Those that voice opposition to the mood of the mourners on these occasions become themselves the targets of vilification. The BBC's Kate Adie was criticised because her reports from Dunblane were deemed too detached, factual and lacking obvious empathy. Similarly, after the death of the Queen Mother in 2002, the BBC presenter Peter Sissons was vilified in some quarters for simply wearing a brown tie when making the announcement. We saw this kind of compassionate policing at its most acute after the death of Diana. No Diana jokes or criticism of the woman were allowed on the media, anything tasteless or offensive was similarly taken off the air or magazine shelves.

It was not surprising that the mood of ostentatious caring ran so high at this time. Diana was herself an icon of conspicuous compassion. She was a very public supporter of good causes such as the campaign to ban land mines, help cancer patients, bulimics and anorexics, stop war in Bosnia and Angola, cure Aids, and so on. She was a professional 'victim'—of infidelity and eating orders—and wore her heart on her sleeve. She was, as Professor Anthony O'Hear put it, the symbol of a 'New Britain in which the mother of the future King publicly weeps at the funeral of a vulgar and self-publicising Italian dress designer'.[3]

The mob was in no mood to tolerate those who failed to show unambiguous empathy. The Scottish Football Association was lambasted for not holding minute's silences at its games. Professor Anthony O'Hear was later rounded upon by the tabloids when in the book *Faking It* he criticised the Diana phenomenon as bogus, as the symptom of 'the elevation of feeling, image and spontaneity over reason, reality and restraint'.[4] Peter Luff, Conservative MP for Mid-Worcestershire, summed up the mood: 'He would have been well advised to have kept his views to himself so soon after her death'.[5] The Queen became a focus of ire too. The crowd simply could not understand the concept of private grief, and demanded that she be seen in public crying too. 'Where are your feelings Ma'am?' howled the tabloids. 'Unless the Queen shows some emotion, we'll soon have a republic' they barked.

'I am a passionate royalist,' said one grandmother from Surrey who went to join the mourners outside Buckingham Palace, 'but I feel so ashamed every time I look towards Buckingham Palace and see that they still haven't lowered the flag to half-mast. All we want is a sign that the royals are suffering like the rest of us'. When the Queen did bow down to their demands, there was relief. 'Now we know the royals are as frail as the rest of us', said one student from South London. 'It is important for the sake of the two princes that they don't bottle up their grief'.[6] The fact that princes William and Harry shed not a public tear at their mother's funeral is the greatest indictment of the public's behaviour at that time. Here were two boys who had suddenly lost their mother at a particularly vulnerable age, showing immense dignity and fortitude amid a multitude of bawling, gaping ghouls.

Private Eye lampooned the media's opportunistic reaction to her death—to the dismay of many. The beginning of its 'Daily Gnome' editorial captures the media's contrived reaction.

> In recent weeks (not to mention the last ten years) we at the Daily Gnome, in common with all other newspapers, may have inadvertently conveyed the impression that the late Princess of Wales was in some way a neurotic, irresponsible and manipulative troublemaker who had repeatedly meddled in political matters that did not concern her and personally embarrassed Her Majesty The Queen by her Mediterranean love-romps with the son of discredited Egyptian businessman.

> We now realise as of Sunday morning that the Princess of Hearts was in fact the most saintly woman who has ever lived, who, with her charitable activities...

In response, several retail chains and individual shops refused to sell *Private Eye*. The magazine lost thousands of sales. Many readers wrote in to register their disgust or cancel their subscriptions.

Yet others were relieved to discover that they were not alone, and that they too had found the public reaction disconcerting, alarmed at this outbreak of 'floral fascism'. The *Guardian*'s Isabel Hilton felt that 'if a powerful demagogue had arisen from the crowd, they would have stormed the palace gates.' Ian Jack, editor of *Granta* magazine, which devoted an issue to 'people who felt differently', took issue with this 'recreational grief'—grief-lite which was actually undertaken as an enjoyable event, much like going to a football match or the last night of the Proms.[7]

For those who 'felt differently' there was a fear that this spectacle would never end. To their relief, and to their vindication, it did. Today, Diana is a mostly forgotten individual. Certainly, judging by the 'outpourings of grief' in late 1997, one would have thought her memory would have remained etched on the public's consciousness. Yet, on the fifth anniversary of her death, the gardens of Althorp and Kensington Palace were deserted. Diana had served her purpose. The public had moved on. They were now too busy 'never forgetting' other dead people.

In 1998, crowds of people lit candles in London's Trafalgar Square to commemorate the life of Linda McCartney, vegetarian campaigner and wife of a pop star. Hours of television coverage and acres of newsprint were devoted to her, with prayers held in school assemblies and her death even mentioned in parliament. Attention was also devoted in that year to the murderers of the toddler Jamie Bulger, as it was after the killing of the schoolgirl Sarah Payne in 2000. In 1999, the television presenter Jill Dando was shot dead on her doorstep in Fulham, West London, prompting yet another spate of regurgitated clichés. 'I can think of only one other occasion when I've felt the same numbing shock as I did yesterday morning when told of Jill Dando's death', wrote the *Mirror*'s Sue Carroll. 'It was the day Princess Diana was killed ... If Diana was the People's Princess then Jill was the People's Presenter'.[8]

Later that year there were huge headlines mourning the death of Helen Rollason, the BBC sports presenter, with the

Sun announcing 'We'll never forget that smile'.[9] Yet who today even remembers who Helen Rollason was, or spends each day thinking of Jill Dando? By the end of the century, the rituals—candles, tears, commemoration books and clichés—had become standardised. They had done so because they were symptoms of an underlying malaise within society; the string of unfortunate dead individuals had merely become conduits through which to channel it.

This was witnessed at its most fearsome during the Soham incident of 2002. That summer, two girls, Holly Wells and Jessica Chapman, went missing from the village of Soham, Cambridgeshire. Their bodies were discovered in late August. Members of the public subsequently flocked to the Cambridgeshire town, where queues to sign the Book of Condolences at St Andrew's Church were often 100 people deep—many more put their names to virtual books of condolence in cyberspace. Ten thousand bouquets and posies, small toys and teddies carpeted the church grounds. At football and cricket matches, race meetings, in shops and supermarkets and on crowded high streets, members of the public paused for two minutes' silence in their honour. Australian prime minister John Howard sent roses on behalf of the Australian people, while Prince Charles sent two handwritten letters to the girls' parents, saying how he 'agonised' over their loss. David Beckham, the murdered girls' hero, dedicated his first goal of the season to them, and former footballer turned hardman actor Vinnie Jones sent his condolences to Soham Town Rangers. 'I feel totally distraught about these very sad losses', he said.[10] The following summer, the pink 'Soham rose' went on view at the Chelsea Flower Show in permanent floral tribute.[11]

The Soham murders were unquestionably tragic. At the same time, it is almost as distressing to see sections of the public jumping on the grief bandwagon, making a drama out of a crisis. The unfortunate inhabitants of Soham were subjected to hoards of grief tourists. The streets jammed over the bank holiday weekend of August 2002 with cars and coaches taking 'visitors' to see nearby Ely Cathedral or the 'sights' of Cambridge where the girls disappeared. The vicar of Soham, the Rev. Timothy Alban-Jones, even heard of a couple who went into a Soham baker's to demand: 'We've seen the church and we're not going home until we've seen the college [where Ian Huntley, the man accused of the double murder, was caretaker]'.

The people of Soham were being used. According to Mr Alban-Jones, the 'tragedy put people in touch with their own hurt'. The letters he received from the public, he said at the time, 'would begin by expressing horror at the tragedy, but then they would go on to talk about things that had happened in their own lives'.[12] Unsurprisingly, on the first anniversary of the murders, the families of the girls asked well-wishers to stay away from the Cambridgeshire town.[13]

But would they have come anyway?

Soham proved particularly potent because it centred on the one subject that most arouses irrational fears and anger: child abuse. As we shall see, when the crowd is in the mood for collective caring, mob violence will invariably follow. A society that feels it normal to send flowers to perfect strangers will also feel it acceptable to throw stones at them too.

3

Nonce-sense

When members of the general public use the death of strangers to forge social bonds, it follows that a highly charged mob will transform 'sorrow' into anger. Conspicuous compassion dictates that grief will turn into grievance and grievance into vengeance.

In July 2000, the *News of the World* published the names and whereabouts of all 110,000 of the country's child-sex offenders, along with the summaries of their crimes. The newspaper's stated intention was to seek transparency; that parents would benefit from knowing if a sex offender lived in their area. Yet, by listing those who had raped or murdered children alongside those who had merely downloaded pictures of girls only slightly younger than those whose breasts are exposed in the same newspaper, the *News of the World*'s editor Rebekah Wade did a disservice to lesser sex offenders. As Tom Utley pointed out in the *Daily Telegraph*: 'All hope of re-acceptance into society, all hope of living down his shame, stripped away, not by law, but by her whim'.[1] One newspaper's compassionate crusade begat cruel outcomes.

Soon afterwards, in the Paulsgrove estate in Portsmouth, a protest that targeted a convicted 'named and shamed' paedophile turned into a mini-riot. A paediatrician had the word 'Paedo' scrawled in white paint all over her house by illiterate hate-carers in South Wales, who had misunderstood the sign at her surgery. When a *Sunday Telegraph* reporter asked neighbours what they thought of this attack, they were unrepentant. 'I heard that doctor's house had got attacked, but it's because people don't want no paedophiles here,' said one mother of three. 'If you've got children like me, then you can understand why people are worried about

15

perverts.' Another woman agreed: 'It's bad that someone innocent's house has been attacked, but what will happen if they're not all locked up'.[2]

During the trial of the Soham suspects in August 2002, bystanders gathered outside Peterborough Magistrates Court to hurl abuse at Maxine Carr, who was charged with perverting the course of justice in relation to the double murder. Baying women and burly men holding 'Rot in Hell Forever' placards slammed eggs at the police van carrying Carr, screaming 'sick cow' and 'evil bitch'.[3] Meanwhile, terrified children, who had been taken to participate in this festival of hate-caring, looked on crying. The participants in this unedifying spectacle undoubtedly believed that they were doing the correct, 'caring' thing. Two children had been murdered and people were at Peterborough, ostensibly, to express their anger at this crime. Yet it suspiciously appeared to be an excuse for a good, adrenaline-fuelled day out—a chance to prove one's 'humane' credentials in the comfort of the crowd. Yet Carr had not at that stage actually been convicted of anything. Just because she was eventually found guilty in assisting Ian Huntley, this does not legitimise such actions. She was, at that point, technically innocent.

Over the last ten years, many innocents have suffered at the hands of the compassionate lynch mob. Frank Revill, now 61, of Folkestone, Kent was such a victim. In 1997, rumours spread that a child abuser was to move into his neighbourhood. After he was spotted unloading belongings into a house belonging to his daughter, he received verbal abuse, had windows smashed and was subjected to threatening telephone calls. In the West Midlands, a 14-year-old girl died after a firebomb attack on a house intended for a paedophile. In February 1997, Manchester pensioner Francis Duffy was beaten and severely injured after being mistaken for a child abuser called Brynley Dummet, whose picture had been printed by the *Manchester Evening News* three months earlier. Paul Webster, aged 38 of Plymouth, drank himself to death after neighbours accused him of being a child abuser. Webster, who had been giving children guitar lessons, was threatened with a knife and harassed for three weeks, with 'Beware nonce lives here' sprayed on his flat door.[4] Paradoxically, those who 'care' about the deaths of innocents actually cause the deaths of more innocents. The 'paediatrician' attack was so memorable not just for its comedy value, but for its irony; that an ignorant attempt to protect 'the kids' lead to an attack on someone who genuinely does help children.

In the long term, anti-paedophile hysteria promotes fear and suspicion. Every year 120,000 parents are subjected to the ordeal of being wrongly abused of child abuse.[5] In December 2002, Edinburgh City Council announced plans to ban parents from taking video recordings of their children's Nativity plays without the consent of the whole cast, lest images fall into the hands of paedophiles who may put them on the internet. A month later, police sent round 12 officers, including a detective superintendent, to arrest Pete Townshend on suspicion of possessing, making and inciting the distribution of indecent images of children.[6] It was as if they were going to tackle a gang of armed robbers rather than an ageing rock guitarist.

Our 'caring' attitude means that parents will not let their children walk to school, or permit them play unaccompanied in the street or park. Deprived of exercise, today's children are fatter and unhealthier than ever, and more prone to develop hyperactivity disorders (thus hampering their education). Our 'compassionate' attitude towards 'the kids' is transforming them into prisoners of their own homes, who are never taught how to deal with the world unaided or cross the road by themselves. Kiddie compassion is bad for the kids.

And in many respects, our fears are unfounded. About eight children a year are murdered outside the home in the UK, compared with 50 inside.[7] According to a Unicef study of 2002, American children are almost three times as likely to die at the hands of a stranger than British ones, while even in New Zealand the danger to minors in this regard is twice the level of the UK's.[8] Nor has the danger increased over time. According to one study, between 1988 and 1999 the number of children in the UK murdered between the ages of five and 16 actually dropped from four per million to three per million; the figure for the under-fives fell from 12 per million to nine per million. Cases of abduction in which the offender was found guilty fell from 26 to eight over the same period.[9] Never have children been safer. Despite the facts, fear abounds, and with this fear people seek to demonstrate that they are doing something to address the 'paedophile problem'.

In July 2001, Channel 4 broadcast a one-off special of the programme *Brass Eye*, a spoof current affairs show and brainchild of the satirist Chris Morris. This particular episode centred on a phoney anti-paedophile campaign, in which Morris and his collaborators had devised an anti-child-abuse scheme called 'Nonce Sense'. They interviewed several celebrities, who believed they were endorsing a genuine anti-paedophile crusade. The likes of Gary Lineker, Barbara Follett, Richard Blackwood and Lord Coe were seen backing this transparently ludicrous campaign. Capital Radio DJ Dr Fox was told to repeat to the camera the findings that child abusers have genes in common with crabs. 'That is a scientific fact', he read from the script. 'There is no real evidence for it but it's a scientific fact'. Phil Collins held up a T-shirt that read Nonce Sense. 'Nonce Sense,' he said, 'I'm talking Nonce Sense'. We should not be surprised. In their desire to display their compassionate credentials, celebrities are prone to talk nonsense.

Although *Brass Eye* was excessive in parts, it did prove an important point: when it comes to paedophilia, we prefer gesture over thought, intuition over reason. The *Daily Mail*'s enraged reaction—'THE SICKEST TV SHOW EVER'[10]— was in true keeping with unthinking, conformist 'anti-paedophile' sentiment. Like the celebrities *Brass Eye* lampooned, the tabloids were too eager to be seen as compassionate to see through Morris' very legitimate and ultimately vindicated pranks.

4

Silence of the Critics

One of the most audible, or should we say inaudible, manifestations of the 'care bore' compulsion is the cult of minute's silences to commemorate the dead. Not that it remains a solitary minute's silence. It has now become two minutes, even three and occasionally ten. They are getting longer and we are having more of them, because we want to be seen to care—and increasingly are compelled to do so.

The tradition of observing silent commemoration is centuries old. France lays claim to inaugurating this tradition to honour its fallen heroes in the nineteenth century, but it gained wider cultural currency the following century. A ceremonial silence was observed in most places in the United States to mourn the sinking of the *Titanic* and the *Maine* at noon on 16 April 1912. Soon afterwards, the two-minute silence to remember those that had died in the First World War was introduced in 1919.[1] For the bulk of the twentieth century in Britain, the minute's silence was observed on sporting occasions, normally to remember the death of a national figure or someone connected to the club. The two-minutes silence was reserved to honour those who had died fighting for their country.

Yet periods of silence have become more frequent and lengthy over the last 15 years. For instance, three minutes' silence was observed through the European Union on 14 September 2001, in remembrance of those who were killed in the terrorist attacks three days earlier. In Britain, 12 months later, fellow pupils of Milly Dowler gathered for a five-minute silence in memory of the murdered schoolgirl.[2] Does this mean the 9/11 disaster was three times as bad as the Titanic disaster, or that the horrible death of a innocent girl was five times as tragic? Of course it shouldn't. (Although in the case of Milly Dowler's friends, this was a semi-personal tragedy, so we must put this gesture into context.)

It does not stop here. In October 1999, mourners attending a mass at St Michael and All Angels Church in West London to commemorate the Ladbroke Grove crash, held a five-minute silence.[3] In 1993, more than 1,000 anti-racist demonstrators marching through London's East End held a ten-minute vigil in honour of an Asian who had been beaten up by eight white men.[4] Children at a Newcastle similarly observed a ten-minute silence in February 2001 to raise money for cancer research.[5]

There is seemingly a case of compassion inflation, with individuals and organisations seeking to prove how much more they care by elongating the silences. This is a reaction to the minute's silence being practised so frequently. It is as if by extending these periods, there is competition to prove who is more empathetic. When a group called Hedgline calls for a two-minute silence to remember all the 'victims' whose neighbours have grown towering hedges,[6] we truly have reached the stage where this gesture has been emptied of meaning.

As the author has found out, anybody who voices unease at this exponential growth will feel the anger of the crowd. In the wake of Soham, there were periods of silence held not just in football stadia on Saturday, but being an August bank holiday weekend, for games on Monday too. I happened to be at games in the Nationwide Second Division on both occasions. When the second one was announced on the Monday, I muttered to a friend: 'Oh for Christ's sake'. A fan of the same team in front of me turned round, glared at me, and with an outstretched finger asked aggressively: 'What did you say?' He was in no mood for dissent, so I kept quiet. 'Watching footballers huddle and bow their heads before this week's matches', wrote one Manchester United fan in *The Times* in September 2002, 'it occurred that, with football having taken the place of organised religion, scarcely a match seems to kick off without an obligatory minute's silence.'[7]

Football used to be regarded at best as an exercise that embodied masculinity and stoicism. At worst, it was associated with the worst elements of machismo excess and yobbishness—in the 1980s it was a slum game watched by slum people played in slum stadiums. Those days seem far off now. Emotionalism has crept into the game, to the degree that Paul Merson and Tony Adams are applauded for crying in front of the cameras upon confessing to having addiction problems. And today it is where the cult of ghoulish mourning sickness can be experienced as a grand spectacle.

In the wake of the 1971 Ibrox disaster in Glasgow, and to a lesser extend, the Hillsborough disaster of 1989, there was no mass outpouring of grief. There was rightly much anger at why such calamities were allowed to happen. Yet, were a disaster of the same magnitude to happen today, we would be subjected to weeks of teddy bears, scarves and crying in public.

In June 2003, the Manchester City midfielder Marc-Vivien Foé died suddenly while playing an international game for Cameroon in the Confederations Cup. An unexpected tragedy for a young man was transformed into a media spectacle. The BBC news website was inundated with countless tributes, as was one of Manchester City's fanzine messageboards, all expressing their deepest personal shock at this tragedy—from Gutted of Middlesbrough to Profoundly Upset of Brighton and Hove Albion. Fifa announced a plan to rename the Confederations Cup in his name, while Manchester City itself 'retired' its 23 shirt in his honour.

Yet, these were not particularly noble gestures. The Confederations Cup is a much-criticised competition and one has the suspicion that Fifa might have benefited from having Foé's name attached to it. Nor is the Manchester City number 23 shirt much coveted, it being the normal preserve of substitutes, mid-season signings and on-loan players. It is not the same as 'retiring' one's number 7 shirt —this would actually be a meaningful sacrifice, not just a cheap gesture.

No one questions it was a tragedy for the man, his family, friends and possibly Manchester City and Cameroon fans, but as we have seen in society at large, there are always those who want to muscle in on the grieving process. The electronic messages are never anonymous. Fans of, say, Aston Villa or Hartlepool, always want to make it known where the sympathy is coming from. Indeed, football fanzine websites[8] are routinely inundated with messages of condolence—not just for old players. Following the demise of Joe Strummer from The Clash in 2002 and the death the following year of an actress from *Holby City*, one Queen's Park Rangers ezine featured many postings from fans expressing sorrow. What exactly has this to do with football? And how authentic is this in the first place? In terms of Manchester City fans, are these the same ones who routinely refer to Manchester United as 'the Munichs' (after the Munich air disaster of 1958 that killed most of a young United team)?

Like paedophile-hunting or Diana-mourning, the custom of inflated minutes' silence is a cultural phenomenon that feeds on the mob mentality and the desire for conformity. It betrays the hallmarks of a society not 'in touch with its emotions' but one that is intolerant of dissent. In November 1938, Turkey held a three-minute silence as a tribute to the death of leader Ataturk. In 1953, following the death of Stalin, there was a compulsory five-minute silence held behind the Iron Curtain.[9] There is no reason to embrace a ritual that is the trademark of dictatorships. Surrendering ourselves to the impassioned crowd, letting ourselves be ruled by emotion rather than intellect—these are the characteristics of fascism. Far from demonstrating how 'caring' we are, these periods of silence resemble the two minutes of hate the citizens of *Nineteen-eighty-four* were compelled to perform.

5

Lapel Louts

One of the most visible symptoms of the culture of ostentatious caring is the proliferation of empathy ribbons. Today one can view, purchase and wear empathy ribbons for a plethora of causes—to show that you support cancer victims/ children maimed by landmines/ soldiers shot during the First World War for cowardice. Ostensibly, these are designed to 'raise awareness' and much-needed funds, which will go to saving lives and helping the needy. Yet, this strategy has not worked. The growing trend for sporting ribbons has not actually brought about a tangible increase in donations to charities, and certainly not one in proportion to the growth of ribbons. It would seem that wearing that loop is not really concerned with 'raising awareness' but more about individuals projecting their ego onto society. It's a semiotic device to announce: 'I care—deeply'.

The original version of the empathy ribbon was the red Aids loop, introduced in 1991 at the Toni Awards ceremony in New York. More than 100 million of these have since been distributed worldwide, spawning variations (in Scotland, the Aids awareness ribbon is tartan) and myriad imitators, perhaps the best known being the pink version for breast cancer. Elsewhere, dark blue in Britain is for ME awareness, but borne in the United States it signifies 'total freedom on the Internet'. Mauve is for animal rights, yellow is for 'I want someone home'—usually a political prisoner or hostage. Green ribbons are worn by supporters of Sinn Féin, although in 1997 they were also sported by professional golfers in sympathy with a caddie who had developed leukaemia. Pale blue can either mean solidarity with anti-drink-driving campaigners or a mysterious group called

'Coventry Community Safety Team 1996'. The colours of the rainbow indicate sympathy for gay and lesbian Scots. Those grieving for Princess Diana got their own ribbon. André Agassi and Greg Rusedski started a brief trend of wearing black ribbons to commemorate her. With the proliferation of many empathy ribbons, confusion is understandable. One might assume that someone with a green ribbon supports Irish republicans or golfers, but he could easily be supporting organ donors or empathising with the victims of ovarian cancer. An orange ribbon is not, as one might suspect, to declare solidarity with Ulster loyalists, but rather to support racial tolerance or safety on the US highways. Royal blue can be child abuse or for better water quality; grey for urban violence or brachial plexus; and white for the right to life, diabetes and Alzheimer's.[1] Red Ribbon International (RRI) is regularly asked for advice on ribbon identification, because a lot of people initially assumed that all loops were Aids-related. 'We had a lot of trouble with black ribbons', said Mike Campling, director of RRI, in 1997. 'Many people thought it was something to do with black people and Aids'.[2] Yet even HIV charities have become the victim of confusion, as those raising awareness for substance abuse or epidermolysis bullosa also sport the red ribbon.

Still, the cause of Aids remains the most popular, it being associated with pop stars and Hollywood stars. On the face of it, concern is justified. By 2003, the Aids virus had claimed the lives of 15 million Africans. At the same time, two million Africans get tuberculosis every year, yet spending on AIDS research exceeds spending on tuberculosis by a factor of 90 to one.[3] More than five million Africans die each year from malaria and another five million from diarrhoea.[4] Diarrhoea is far more cheaply remedied, yet, as P.J. O'Rourke once observed, you don't see folks in the West wearing brown ribbons. There is simply no compassionate kudos to be gained from it.

Ribbons very much celebrate the cult of victimhood so characteristic of the post-Diana consensus. They are designed even to turn soldiers, formerly heroes, into victims. During the Second Gulf War of 2003, the *News of The World* launched a yellow ribbon campaign backed by Tony Blair and the Defence Secretary, Geoff Hoon, 'to honour ALL our troops in the Gulf'. According to the newspaper, two million Britons followed its call.[5] If you do not want to be perceived as a militarist, there is the white poppy, designed to declare pacifism or to commemorate those shot for cowardice during conflicts.

Even the traditional red poppy has suffered. It used to be sported in November, in the days leading to Remembrance Sunday. Yet they are now routinely seen in October. There is almost an unspoken competition, particularly among politicians, to see who can been seen wearing it the earliest. In 2002 for instance, Tony Blair and his colleagues were seen wearing poppies on October 23.[6] Not only are they sprouting earlier and earlier, they are getting larger by the year. This is notable among members of the Royal Family, who demonstrate their status at the apex of the hierarchy of compassion today by sporting veritable bouquets of poppies, or extra large versions. One might argue that this is their prerogative, in that many of the Windsors hold positions in the forces, and that many of them have served, fought and died in them. But so have millions of Britons, who feel no need to resort to such show-off behaviour. This is a reaction to compassion inflation and competition for lapel space. Supporters of servicemen feel this a necessary course of action in a market now teeming with the more familiar looped empathy ribbon.

A variation of lapel loutism is the habit of wearing plastic red noses once every two years to show awareness for BBC Red Nose day—or in the case of some taxi drivers, having a large plastic nose on the front of one's cab the whole year round. The flowering of empathy ribbons has occurred in tandem with the cult of charity cards. People increasingly send Christmas cards bought from charities, with the cause in question modestly but definitely imprinted at the bottom of it.[7]

It would be flippant to sneer wholly at the desire to raise awareness of good causes—were it not for the fact its effectiveness in doing so is not particularly evident. Between 1995 and 1999, the era that saw the flowering of empathy ribbons, donations to good causes dropped by 31 per cent, according to the pressure group the National Council for Voluntary Organisations. In 1995, the average monthly donation to charity from an individual was £12, by the next year it was £10 and in 1997 it had fallen to £9.60. In 1999, while nine out of ten people said it was important to donate to charity, fewer than half of those questioned had actually made any donations.[8] At the time of writing, donations to charity are on the rise again. Britons gave £7.3 billion to good causes in 2002, up £400 million on 2001. Over the same period, however, the actual number of Britons giving fell, from 69 to 63 per cent of the population.[9] At best, the jury is still out as to whether the habit of wearing empathy ribbons has 'raised awareness'.

This can only lead to the suspicion that empathy ribbons are designed principally to communicate to strangers one's political, social and possibly sexual leanings. Wearing a ribbon is far easier than working for charity and consistently giving money to it. It is merely a cheap method for an individual to appear oh-so benevolent to one's friends, peers and fellow countrymen.

6

Animal Wrongs

An old maxim goes that the British are a nation of animal lovers. Certainly, in recent decades we have become a nation of very belligerent animal lovers. Observe the swell in popularity of the anti-fox-hunting movement, the appearance of protesters campaigning outside vivisection clinics, or the popularity of vegetarianism. Since the 1960s, and particularly since the 1990s, the animal rights movement has flourished. Alongside the long-established League Against Cruel Sports and the British Union for the Abolition of Vivisection, recent years have witnessed the establishment and ascendancy of Stop Huntingdon Animal Cruelty, Viva, Animal Aid, the British branch of the People for the Ethical Treatment of Animals (PETA) and the extremist Animal Liberation Front.

This, so animal rights apologists assert, is a good thing. It proves that we have cultivated a more humane and progressive attitude to all living things. The statistics ostensibly back this assertion. A Mori poll of December 2002 showed that 80 per cent of Britons believed that hunting with dogs was cruel.[1] Another Mori poll commissioned by the *New Scientist* magazine in 1999 showed that 64 per cent of the public were also against animal experimentation.[2]

All the above, however, is misleading. It does not prove that we have become more humane in regards to animals. It merely betrays how we have developed a sentimental, hypocritical and mushy-headed attitude to living things. We live in a country in which one person will in the morning happily tuck into a breakfast of bacon and sausages, and in the evening watch *Babe*, a weepy, anthropomorphic film about a the adventures of a pig—or delight in the real-life frolics of 'Butch' and 'Sundance', two swine who in January

1998 escaped from an abattoir in Tamworth (their esca-
pades have been made into a BBC film). The British live in
a state of cognitive dissonance when it comes to animals.
For instance, 96 per cent of the British public eat meat.[3]
That is to say, while 64 per cent of the public believes
killing animals for scientific research is wrong, only four per
cent (at best) believe killing them for their meat is unac-
ceptable. If we really were a nation of animal lovers, we
would focus our energies on slaughterhouses—or 'abattoirs'
as they are euphemistically called—rather than hunt
gatherings or vivisection centres.

The number of animals who die on a hunt or in a clinic
pale into comparison to the number that are slaughtered,
often cruelly, for consumption. For instance, each year in
the USA, over 100 million mammals and five billion birds
are slaughtered for consumption.[4] In the UK, 600 million
broiler chickens, 15 million pigs, four million lambs and
three million cattle are killed annually for the purposes of
consumption.[5] To put this in perspective, the average Briton
in their lifetime will consume 550 poultry, 36 pigs, 36 sheep
and 8 oxen. During the same lifetime, four animals will be
sacrificed for the purposes of vital medical research—these
being mainly mice and rats. The equivalent number of foxes
killed by hunts will be 0.02.[6]

It is not just about quantity, but quality. Your hunted
wild animal or laboratory animal will enjoy an existence
incomparably better than that of creatures reared for
consumption. Consider the life of broiler chickens in Britain
today. They are housed in large, windowless sheds that can
contain between 20,000 and 50,000 birds. Each bird is
allocated a space about the size of an A4 sheet of paper,
living on a diet of recycled blood, offal and feathers of dead
birds. They are collected by catchers who move through the
sheds, holding several birds upside down by their legs,
cramming them into crates that are loaded into lorries.
Dislocated hips, bruising and broken wings and legs are
common. Thanks to the suffocating conditions that veer
between extreme cold and heat, around six million birds die
en route to the slaughterhouse. There, the still-living are
hung upside-down and shackled by their feet to a moving

line, that takes them to an electric bath to render them unconscious. The line then moves the chicken to a neck-cutter where the birds are bled for a 90 seconds before entering a scalding tank. Yet poorly carried out stunning and neck cutting means many of the birds are still alive when entering the scalding tank—one study put the proportion at 25 per cent.

Most pigs are reared under similarly intensive conditions and are killed by first being stunned, by having tongs placed on either side of the neck behind the ears. Because the tongs are often held in the wrong place or for too short a time or the slaughterhouse uses inadequate voltage, pigs often are not adequately stunned. Many regain consciousness before throat slitting. As it approaches the slaughterhouse, the pig smells blood and starts to panic and squeal. Its handlers often respond by hitting it with an iron pipe until it is restrained on the conveyor belt. In Denmark, a preferred method of slaughter is suffocation through carbon dioxide, which causes breathlessness and hyperventilation among pigs trying to escape.

Similarly, in Britain most cattle are slaughtered by having first been stunned by a captive bolt pistol, then by having their throats cut. However the bolt does not always successfully stun the animal. The most common failure is improper positioning of the bolt to the head, a problem accentuated when cattle are agitated and struggle to escape. Mis-stunning can cause distress and often means the animal is still alive during throat cutting. Sheep in the UK are similarly killed by electric stunning followed by neck-cutting. Again, the process is not always effective and the lamb may regain consciousness before throat-slitting.[7]

We are not routinely reminded of these facts. Most omnivores simply do not want to know. If they did, they would fear they might have to make an effort to change their own lifestyles. When voices of protest are raised against the meat industry, it is primarily directed against Jewish and Muslim methods of slaughter. In June 2003, for instance, the Farm Animal Welfare Council made a proposal to outlaw ritual slaughter, recommending that all animals be stunned by electric shock or have a bolt fired to the head prior to any cutting. Yet there is evidence that the Jewish method of slaughter is actually less stressful to animals. Under kosher laws, cattle are slaughtered by having the carotid artery severed, causing immediate loss of blood so that the pressure in the brain falls dramatically, leading to almost immediate unconsciousness in the animal.[8] As with moves to ban vivisection or fox-hunting, the campaign to outlaw ritual religious slaughter is an example of the majority of Britons demanding that others change their behaviour, not their own. It is the triumph of gesture over action.

So what of those who bellow that fox hunting is 'barbaric'? Unlike the thousands of animals who will die clumsy deaths for consumption, the fox hunted to death by hounds will die a swift death. The alternatives to hunting, such as poisoning or shooting, are far crueller in dealing with this rural pest. So why the fuss over the issue? If not the function of soppy, fuzzy-headedness, the anti-hunting lobby is fuelled simply by class resentment. As one left-wing writer admits:

> This has nothing to do with foxes. It's a glorious bit of class war... No Labour MP is going to worry about fishing, because there is nothing objectionable about anglers. But there is immense pleasure to be had from thwarting the fun of people who go hunting.[9]

And what of a those who decry testing on animals as 'cruel'? Well, vivisection has been responsible for making countless medical advances, from insulin to treat diabetes, polio vaccines, antibiotics, safe anaesthetics, open heart surgery, organ transplantation, hip replacements and drug treatments for ulcers, asthma and high blood pressure. To ban the 'cruel' practice of vivisection would be very cruel indeed for sick human beings. The vast majority of animals tested on aren't sweet bunny rabbits or doe-eyed dogs, but rats and mice. 'But they're just like us!' the anti-vivisectionists will continue to cry. Well, speak for yourselves.

Two-thirds of the British public in 1999 said they were against experimentation on animals for medical purposes, according to a *New Scientist* poll. Yet, when this was conducted with the question rephrased, with a preface mentioning that research using animals is making progress into finding the cure for Aids and into better treatment for leukaemia, 45 per cent (including the 'don't knows', a majority) now said they backed vivisection. This leads to the unfortunate conclusion that many people assume scientists experiment on animals, and thus risk being killed by animal rights extremists, for the sheer fun of it. Vivisection is a necessary procedure that has saved and can save the lives of human beings; rural foxes are a pest that need to be culled. Yet we don't need to eat meat. Vegetarianism may bring up dietary problems, but it can be healthier than omnivorism if practised responsibly—certainly healthier than the carnivorous fast-food diet practised by a sizeable and oversized proportion of the population today. Personally, I do not subscribe to the oxymoronic philosophy of animal rights or believe that eating animals is actually wrong, nor am I deluded by today's Disneyfied view of animals. I simply say that the way we rear and kill animals for consumption at present is cruel and neglected.

The campaign for reform of the meat industry is overshadowed by more exciting, emotive issues. These provide for far greater opportunities to bond with one's fellow man, to wave placards of bunny rabbits with electrodes stuck to their heads, or the thrill of out-foxing posh people on horses on a bright day in the countryside. As Keith Tester argued in his *Animals and Society*, militant opponents of vivisection and radical animal liberation advocates are not primarily concerned with the creatures they profess to defend. Rather, they are misanthropes driven by the urge to seize the moral high ground above fellow human beings.[10] To urge a total rethink on the meat industry would involve far too much effort and sincere, clear-thinking. It would involve changing the world and altering one's own lifestyle, rather than indulging in emoting and sloganeering.

7

Any Spare Change?

In a letter to the *Independent* in November 1997, a reader noted: 'For 35 years I lived in towns such as Norwich, St Albans and Swindon without seeing a single beggar. Begging was something which happened in the Third World. Then suddenly, within a year or two of the 1987 election, young people began begging on the streets.'[1]

Certainly, the re-emergence of mendicancy was one of the notable features of the Thatcherite period, and to many, one of its defining legacies. The emergence of begging came to symbolise the appalling cost of the doctrine that professed there to be no such thing as society. Ken Livingstone is one adherent to this school of thought. 'The sight of teenagers and old people sleeping in doorways all over the West End of London was a bequest of Margaret Thatcher to the people of London', he says. 'Her policies of cutting benefit rights to groups such as vulnerable teenagers, while housing costs in London rocketed, drove thousands on to the streets or into low-quality housing'.[2]

By inference, because eighties-style selfishness causes homelessness, nineties-style compassion can be the remedy. To many people today, giving alms to beggars is regarded as a noble and necessary thing. 'For the young homeless, personal small acts of kindness can give them hope', says Lorraine Hewitt of London's Stockwell Project. 'Many poor people now rely on such donations as the only alternatives to crime or total destitution.'[3] To the social commentator Joan Smith, it is not merely a matter of simple economics: '[T]he act of giving is a recognition of our shared humanity. Dave told me he hated begging in Tube stations and felt humiliated... What he wanted, even more than the cost of a meal, was a little respect.'[4]

Yet giving money to mendicants may be doing them no favours. Whatever its genesis, the crisis of homelessness will not be solved by giving your spare change. By doing so you could be keeping a beggar on the streets, or at worst, sending him to an early grave. Our so-called caring attitude to the homeless is actually a decidedly cruel one.

Research undertaken by the charity Crisis in 2002 showed that 96 per cent of the homeless are alcoholics or drug addicts.[5] According to the Rough Sleepers Unit, many homeless people can afford to be drug addicts thanks only to money they receive from begging. Studies in Nottingham and Manchester have shown that up to 90 per cent who beg do so to sustain an addiction, and in Brighton almost half those begging have told the police they do so to sustain a habit.[6] There is growing evidence that many beggars are not 'hungry and homeless' at all, that they are housed in day centres, friends' houses or on their own, with the sleeping bags and blankets being merely props.[7] In May 2003, police found that 20 of Middlesbrough city centre's most notorious homeless beggars were nothing of the sort. Housed, they had been taking up to £1,400 a week thanks to donations from the public.[8]

For this reason, many charities have urged us to refrain from giving alms. In September 2000, Victor Adebowale, chief executive of the youth homeless charity Centrepoint, stated that donating to beggars only made matters worse: it helped them to remain on the streets, it gave them less incentive to seek help that was available nearby.[9] Louise Casey, director of the Rough Sleepers Unit, has implored: 'The more difficult, but better option is to help people who are homeless by giving time, goods or money to a registered charity designed to help them in the long term'.[10] 'Giving to beggars—whether homeless or not—is wasted charity as the money always goes on alcohol or drugs', says Frank Owen of the Teesside Homeless Action Group.[11]

In July 2003 the homeless charity Thames Reach Bondway launched a poster campaign to reaffirm this message, with posters reading 'The money you give to those who beg... may even buy the drugs that kill him' and 'Can you spare 20p for a cup of tea? How about £10 for a bag of

heroin? Or £12 for a rock of crack?'[12] 'I never never met a
healthy temporary resident of the street who, once caught,
didn't become a permanent fixture of the night street,
caught not just by drugs and drink', writes John Bird,
founder of the *Big Issue*, 'but by the endless supply of money
from a generous public. The giving public might just as well
have given the beggars poisons to play with.'[13]

If you want to help the homeless, it is better to donate
money to charities rather than individuals, but the conduct
of some charities is also open to question. In 2003 West-
minster City Council complained that the enormous
number of organisations delivering food to rough sleepers in
central London—almost 60 groups—was helping to ensure
that the homeless and vulnerable remained on the streets.

According to left-liberal opinion in Britain, homelessness
and thus mendicancy is the fault of right-wing economics.
Begging is a function of poverty and the triumph of individualism. In some respects, they have a point. The Conservatives closed down many mental health institutions in the
1980s, which emptied thousands of mentally ill individuals
onto the streets who were not able to look after themselves.
Yet they were given succour by the R.D. Laing and
Foucauldian school of thought, which deems the notion of
'madness' a cultural creation and the idea of incarceration
for the mentally ill oppressive. The thinking that 'Care in
the Community' is humane has only increased the misery
of many vulnerable people.

Yet, more culpable than the State's attack on 'society' has
been that on the family unit. The family has fragmented in
the post-1960s consensus, with the encouragement of
'liberal' campaigners and some Home Secretaries through
governmental legislation that has made it harder to be a
two-parent family and easier to be a one-parent unit. As a
Civitas study in 2000 has shown, adults from broken
families are nearly twice as likely as others to end up
homeless.[14] A healthy, close family unit is the best defence
against wayward children ending up on the street.

The notion that begging is a logical symptom of 'selfish'
Thatcherism has to be challenged by historical reality.

Homelessness has grown in part because in the 1970s, police and local authorities stopped enforcing vagrancy laws.[15] In the 1930s for instance, when poverty was greater in real and relative terms, begging was practically unknown. Despite the thousands driven onto the streets by the Depression, beggars were uncommon, as would-be mendicants lived in fear of the Vagrancy Act, which gave a sentence of seven days imprisonment without the option of a fine. This was prior to the establishment of the welfare state, put in place precisely to ensure a safety net for all. Today we have the opposite: a welfare state *and* mendicancy. Nor can it be purely the consequence of poverty. Homelessness grew during the 1980s, just as unemployment fell. At 3.2 million in 1982, unemployment levels now stands at 1.4 million.

This trend is not confined to these shores. According to Hartley Dean, professor of social policy at the University of Luton and editor of *Begging Questions*: 'The re-emergence of begging is associated with global economic trends and is evident in most western cities—dramatically so in the post-communist countries of central and eastern Europe'.[16] This gives us some clue to one of its causes. Eastern Europeans in the post-war era grew up with the understanding that the State was there to provide for them. Suddenly faced with the prospect of individualism, they were rendered helpless. In Britain, the Thatcherite revolution had a similar effect. Britons had been raised with the expectation that the State would hold our hand from the cradle to the grave. Faced with the reality of being liberated from it, many foundered. 'Caring' socialism, whether it be the Stalinist or Attlee variety, rendered individuals mental infants, incapable of looking after themselves without the benign hand of Big Father. The loss of income support in 1988 for 16 and 17 year olds is often cited for increasing homelessness levels at that time,[17] yet it could be said that its existence in the first place was the cause of the problem. It was the welfare state, in seeking to become Big Father, that has helped to break up families in the first place.

There persists today the idea that begging is 'society's problem', from which emerges the conviction that giving alms is a good thing. But this notion has only augmented homelessness. In past times, when the public did not subscribe to the Statist doctrine that 'we are all guilty', beggars felt shame. In our communitarian times, beggars no longer feel shame, we feel guilt. Consequently, giving money to beggars is seen as not only acceptable, but positively virtuous. Yet in Japanese society, for instance, which is still shame- rather than guilt-orientated, homelessness is minimal and begging practically non-existent. On a cultural level, homelessness has grown because there is no longer a taboo on mendicancy. On a political level, it has grown *because* we have a welfare state.

We are told that handing over money gives the homeless a portion of their humanity back. Yet so does talking to them—but this is often a lengthy and demanding process. Far better to chuck them a pound and be on your way. In reality, providing alms to mendicants merely keeps them on the streets. They will spend their alms on drink or drugs. With his warm glow of self-satisfaction, only the donor benefits.

8

Not in My Name

Anti-war demonstrations are one of the trademarks of the post-war era. They reached their apex in 1968, with mass protests in Britain, France and America in opposition to the Vietnam conflict. Situationists, pacifists and students descended to the streets of London, Paris, San Francisco and beyond. Their aim: to stop the Vietnam war. By registering their disgust at the bloodshed in southeast Asia, these protesters hoped to help to put an end to it. As Tarik Ali and Susan Watkins recall of that famous year of protest: 'Nineteen sixty-eight was an attempt to create a new world, a new starting point for politics, for culture, for personal relations'.[1]

Anti-war protesting in the twenty-first century is rather a different matter. Consider the marches that anticipated the Second Gulf War of 2003, and those held in its duration. Their most memorable feature was the slogan seen on countless placards and badges: 'Not In My Name'. This popular phrase suggests that anti-war protesting is no longer about stopping wars but registering one's personal disapproval of it.

Spiked-online's Brendan O'Neill went on one London anti-war march in November 2002 to gauge the protesters' concerns. Despite being of an anti-war disposition himself, he was not impressed. O'Neill asked: what was the protesters' message for Tony Blair? 'We're here to tell him "not in our name"' said Mark, a 21-year-old student. A woman called Abby agreed. 'We want the government to know that we want nothing to do with their wars'. 'I know there will be an invasion of Iraq and I know there isn't much I can do about it', concurred another, 'But what should I do—stay at home and say nothing? I can still add my voice to the protests.' Others argued that the Government 'would probably ignore' the protests and get on with their wars anyway, 'because that is what governments do'. O'Neill asked Abby what exactly was the point of protesting if it was not going to make any difference. 'We are showing our disapproval and voicing our individual opposition.' Elsewhere in Glasgow, a *Sunday Herald* reporter spotted the placard: 'War on Iraq? Not in my name, not in Dorothy's name'.[2] As O'Neill concluded: 'Anti-war protests are not so much about challenging Bush and Blair and trying to stop them in their tracks, but about expressing an individual, moral revulsion to war'.[3]

Not In My Name? Not in Dorothy's name? Who cares what your name is? Liberated Iraqis had names too, so did those who had been killed and tortured by Saddam Hussein's régime. The slogan 'Not In My Name' is fitting for a generation that comprehends global concerns in terms of choosy consumers. It is a self-important motto for those who regard the world through the prism of passive victimhood that, as the *Guardian*'s Julie Burchill put it, combines a 'mixture of egotism and self-loathing that often characterises recreational depression—an unholy alliance of Oprahism and Meldrewism in which you think you're scum, but also that you're terribly important'.[4]

As with wearing an empathy ribbon, going on demonstrations today is too often an exercise in attention-seeking. At one anti-war protest I witnessed in Dublin in February 2003, there was a placard with the words 'Cyclists Against War'. In London that month a young artist came past marches selling cassettes: 'Artists Against The War'.[5] This is akin to those letters that periodically appear in the *Guardian*, from 'Scientists against Israeli brutality' or 'Children's fiction writers against war'.[6] These preposterous boasts do nothing to lessen conflict and everything to aggrandize one's standing among one's peers.

Anti-war marchers resemble anti-capitalist campaigners, and indeed their numbers are often drawn from the same pool. Yet their goal is even less clear, what with the movement being an unholy alliance of anti-GM protesters,

Kurdish Marxists, green campaigners and car-haters. They know what they are against (capitalism, boo!), yet they are unclear as to what they are for. When I went to see the first May Day march in London in 2000, the ignorance of the protesters was something to behold. 'So, what do you want to replace capitalism with? Green socialism, communitarian collectivisation, a mixed economy?' I asked one. 'Well', he replied, paused, then replied, 'there's got to be *something* better.' Anti-capitalist campaigners possess all the fervour and moral righteousness of old-fashioned Trotskyite activists, but none of the intelligence, ideology or vision. At its most articulate, one leading anti-globalisation collective argues for 'building alternative social and economic structures based on co-operation, ecological sustainability, and grassroots democracy',[7] the kind of words one would expect of Neil from *The Young Ones*. The spoof band Ciderdelic may have been joking when they attended a rally with a banner that read 'Abolish capitalism and replace it with something nicer', but it read as an authentic manifesto.

Even George Monbiot, the doyen of 'anti-globalisers', cannot explain what his movement actually stands for. In the introduction to his *Age of Consent*,[8] after he pronounces himself a member of the 'vast and messy coalition... widely known as the "Global Justice Movement"' he goes on to issue the caveat: 'Most of its participants now reject this term... other people have called it the "Civil Society Movement", the "Anti-Capitalist Movement", the "World Democracy Movement", the "Alternative Globalization Movement" or the "Movement of Movements"'.[9] Such quibbling betrays this so-called movement's immature character, being reminiscent of the internecine squabbles between the People's Front of Judea and the Judean People's Front in Monty Python's *Life of Brian*.

Participating in an anti-capitalist march is much the same as going on an anti-war parade. It is designed to show that you are a nice person, and to register unhappiness with the fact that horrid things happen in the world. At best, anti-capitalist protests resemble carnivals rather than political protests, with the music, flowers, face paint, fancy dress, jugglers and the drinking. At worst, demonstrators behave like over-excitable football supporters: most of the 40 arrested after anti-capitalist riots in Euston, London, in December 1999 were unfit to be charged or questioned because they were still drunk or under the influence of drugs.[10] Anti-globalisation protests resemble today a global, travelling circus.

Perhaps this is not such a new development. As anyone who goes to football matches will tell you, there is something alluring about being part of the crowd, something bonding and empowering. One anti-war placard spotted in Canberra in February 2003 read: 'We are all one',[11] suggesting the campaign for global justice is not the only concern of mass protesters. As Doris Lessing once remarked when recalling her outings at CND marches: 'It seems to go against the grain of left-wing pieties to say that few things are more enjoyable than marching, picketing, striking, rioting; to be part of a large crowd high on singing, chanting, slogans. To be, by definition, with the forces of good against evil. No wonder it is so popular. But is it always, or even often, effective?'[12]

9

You've got Junk Mail

When the internet emerged in the mid-1990s, it was heralded as a device that would bring the world closer together. And this it has, but not merely in a conventional manner of someone in Berlin befriending someone from Birmingham. It has also brought people together to campaign on issues, or to grieve with strangers. It has become a vehicle through which to display one's humanity and tenderheartedness.

The most familiar manifestation is the email petition exhorting us to add our names to a worthy cause. There are many types of e-petition, asking us to register our protest at the oppression of women in Afghanistan, America's reluctance to sign the Kyoto agreement or the continued practice of female circumcision in Africa. Since the beginning of the 'war on terror', however, the most popular cause has been e-petitions campaigning against US militarism. On 10 April 2003, the following arrived in my inbox: 'Moving towards a THIRD WORLD WAR. If you are against this possibility, gathering signatures is an effort to avoid a tragic world event. Your signature may look a minor thing, but many names will help the UN to direct energy in a more peaceful direction.' It had 457 signatures, from citizens of countless countries. Its stated tactic, as with others, was that once a substantial number of signatures are harvested, the e-petition would be submitted to the relevant authority, be it the United Nations, the White House or whatever. But does anybody do so? People who receive such e-petitions simply add their name and then forward it to their friends, who will do the same, ad infinitum. This chain will lead to the creation of a whole new set of petitions, none of which will be sent to the appropriate site of appeal. This is because their purpose has little to do with changing the world. With one click, the individual can prove how benign he is, and with any luck, have strangers from Argentina or Australia spot his name on the petition. Once the e-petition has been forwarded he swiftly puts it in his trash box and then forgets about it ... until the next deserving cause arrives in his inbox.

Email petitions are not only ineffectual, but often based on untruths. One doing the rounds in 1999 urged computer users to make known their alarm at a plan by the Brazilian government to allow an area of Amazonia to be deforested. The problem was that the Brazilian parliamentary proposal in question had actually been defeated, in 1996. Similarly, in 2003 a popular email petition called on the Nigerian government to stop the execution on 3 June that year of a woman convicted of adultery. Issued by the Spanish Branch of Amnesty international, it had collected several million signatures. But it was based on false information. The Nigerian had not been sentenced to death at all. June 3 was not the date of her execution, but the day she was due to come up before a local appeals court.[1] The desire to be seen to care takes precedence over what one is allegedly caring about. Computer users do not take time to look into the facts because they are not really concerned with them. Email petitions are nothing more than glamourised chain letters. They do nothing to stop war or oppression and everything to enrich telecom and electricity companies.

A less ephemeral form of e-caring can be seen not in mail but on websites. Many anti-war petitions sprung up on the web in the approach of the Second Gulf War in 2003, not least on ThePetitionSite.com, devoted to the art of petitions. By 18 July 2003, 1,975 people had signed up to the petition entitled 'No to Bombing Iraq' (although many of this number includes pro-war voices taking exception to the comments of anti-war signatories). Still, this pales by comparison with the 13,315 who had put their names to the 'Incarcerate Kitten Killer' e-petition, which called for the ultimate punishment for a Missouri man who put a seven-week-old cat on a burning barbecue ('Someone should put that jerk in a fire and grill his sorry ass...' exhorts one animal lover).

On ThePetitionSite.com you too can call to 'Stop Goat vivisection', 'Protect Pandas from Exploitation & Display at Las Vegas Casino', 'Stop the open season on B[ritish] C[olumbia] Canada's Grey Wolves' or 'Make pet "owners" into pet "guardians"'. If not animals, you can raise awareness to 'End Nike Sweatshops', 'Feed People, Not Corporations', 'Say no to McUnicef and save children's health!', 'Stop Scrapegoating [sic] Gay/Lesbian Americans For Societal Problems!', 'Strike Down Antiquated Sodomy Laws', 'Save the Eskimos!' or 'Stop Racism in Major League Mascots'. Other threads insist: 'Britain Must Respect the Rights of the Disabled', seek 'Madatory [sic] Life Sentance [sic] for Child Predators' or simply seek to raise awareness of 'Sexual Orientation Rights in Ecuador'. A more conventional and popular pursuit is to express sympathy for the Palestinians victimised by the Israeli authorities.[2] One rarely sees, of course, rallying cries to the effect of 'Lessen taxes for the Middle Classes', 'Clean litter from Our Streets' or 'Greater Vigilance on False Asylum Seekers'. Citizens who are concerned with such matters appreciate the social death that faces anyone who airs such concerns.

The phenomenon of conspicuous compassion is intimately bound to the culture of victimhood. Thus it is unsurprising that websites should be used not just to campaign for the 'oppressed', but to mourn and emote for victims. At commemoratewtc.com, you can not only leave your condolences for the victims of the September 11 attacks, but download your own virtual ribbon 'to honor those most affected by the war in Iraq' and 'attach' it to your own website.[3] Similarly the Long Beach Island sympathy book[4] remains online for those who want to make known their sympathy for those who lost their loved ones on 9/11. Although it features posts from those who actually lost relations on that day, a greater number are from those who were not personally bereaved. Thus the following (all reproduced in verbatim): 'even though we are on the other-side of the world i have become very friendly with lots of americans.my heart & soul is with all those affected by this terrible act.you have my prayers & condolences'. There are others from Dublin ('Good bless all the people that lost one of there love ones. We are thinking of you every day.'), Italy ('I would Like to offer my condolence to those who lost any family or friends during September 11th attacks,I don't know anyone who was affected directly but I have a very good friend of mine in LBI and during that tragic day my heart was there for her') and England ('its been exactly a year ago 2day since this tragedy happened, and you know, i still cry, i didnt lose n e 1 i knew but i lost every1 else, i may not of known them but they were still one of us, going about our usual business, they didn't deserve it.'). Another constant is extreme claims of empathetic distress, such as this from 'Christinia' of New Jersey: 'Every month on the 11th, i stop and say a silent prayer for all the people who lost their lives on september 11th. I will never forget each and every one of them.'

This is also characteristic in the world of blogs. A blog, short for 'web log', is a diary kept on the internet by an individual, in which the blogger relates in cyberspace his or her thoughts—whether they be personal or political or whatever. When a blogger announces that his dad or friend or dog has died, his comments section gets overloaded with expressions of sympathy from perfect strangers. The same is apparent when the bloggers die themselves. The site often lives on as a 'memorial' where one can post comments about what that blogger 'meant to me'. For instance, here 'xokatiepie' expresses condolences for the death of a blogger named 'Becky': 'im so terribly sorry for your great loss, i just read the news article and although i didnt know Becky, she seems like such a lovely girl and i'm sure she will be greatly missed.'[5]

According to Christopher Null of the online magazine *Wired News*, 'deathblogs, to coin a term, do seem to offer comfort to those left behind, whether the sites are visited regularly or not'.[6] Similarly, to judge by some posts on September 11 sites, messages from strangers can be comforting. In the words of Jill McGovern of New Jersey on the Long Beach Island sympathy book: 'I lost my husband, Scott, on Sept. 11th and was very touched by your sympathy book. You can never know what it means to read such beautiful words from people who don't even know us.' At the same time, this should not detract from the questions: how authentic are these posts? Why are strangers apparently so easily affected by something that has not personally involved them? Why do people want to be seen to care so desperately?

10

Drop the Slogans

The postcolonial period has witnessed the exponential growth in Third World debt, and in its trail, the emergence of campaigns in the West to 'drop the debt'. The majority of these debts are owed to Western governments and multilateral institutions such as the World Bank and IMF. Thus countless charities, political bodies and celebrities now exhort us to cancel huge loan repayments that are crippling African economies, the source of so much misery for their inhabitants. Chancellor of the Exchequer Gordon Brown has said that cancelling the debt is 'the greatest moral issue of our day' and the 'greatest single cause of poverty and injustice'.[1]

The best known organisation to do so recently was the Drop the Debt movement, the brainchild of various Christian, charitable and humanitarian bodies. Their Jubilee 2000 campaign demanded the cancellation of $214 billion of 'unrepayable' foreign debts owed by 41 of the world's poorest countries, most of them African.[2] In its name, in May 1998, 70,000 campaigners came to Birmingham to form a human chain around the world's most powerful men during the G8 Birmingham summit. In June 1999, their members journeyed to Cologne to do likewise as the G8 met again to discuss proposals to alleviate the Third World debt mountain. By May 2001 the campaign had collected more signatures (24 million) than any other petition before, and from more countries (120).

On the face of it, debt cancellation could help the world's most underprivileged. By 1999, sub-Saharan Africa owed more than £135 billion to Western creditors, who were taking back £5 in debt payments for every £2 they had offered. It is claimed that cancellation of these debts would save the lives of 20 million children and provide education for 90 million women. Ethiopia spends almost half its export earnings on debt service and four times as much on debt as on health care. Ten thousand Ethiopian children die each year of easily preventable diseases.[3]

Western banks should indeed take some responsibility for the debt mountain accrued in Africa, for they did lend recklessly. But culpable too are corrupt African leaders who swindled their own peoples, who fully appreciate this. According to Rosemary Righter of *The Times*, many Africans approached in the street by debt campaigners have simply refused to sign petitions, stating that cancelling the debt would let their rulers off the hook.[4] Of post-war money lent to Third World countries, about a quarter of it went on military spending and 20 per cent was hived off by klepocratic leaders.[5] In Somalia during the 1990s, while the West poured in aid to relieve the 325,000 dying of starvation, the Somalian government was exporting 600,000 sheep in order to buy more weapons to pursue its civil war.[6] In 1999, famine-hit Ethiopia was spending $2 million a day on arms, including several new MiG aircraft, to wage war on Eritrea. In 2002, the Ethiopian government demanded more aid from the West, while still spending half its budget on building up its army.[7] At the beginning of the 1990s, Peru, one of South America's poorest countries, was spending $300 to $400 million to purchase 26 Mirage 2000 fighter planes.[8]

If not using money for further military projects, rulers of many third-world countries used loans to undertake vast projects of self-aggrandisement. Zaïre (now Congo) used loans to erect a trade centre and underground car park in its capital Kinshasa and to build an elaborate airport next to the head of state's native village.[9] As Paul Vallely summed up in his study *Bad Samaritans, First World Ethics and Third World Debt*: 'only a minority of the loans which made up the massive accrual of Third World debt were spent on anything of lasting value'.[10]

Freeing up the debt of such régimes would merely give them the opportunity to go on another massive spending

spree on weaponry. It would be far more constructive to
implement a moratorium on arms buying than a moratorium on debt. As the then International Development
Secretary Clare Short stated in November 1998, the
cancellation of debt risks not only enriching tyrants, but
penalising poor countries and responsible governments.
Flood-devastated Bangladesh, one of the poorest countries
in the world, has little foreign debt. Neither has Malawi.[11]
Uganda and Mozambique have endured years of hardship
to qualify for the partial relief under the Highly Indebted
Poor Countries scheme devised by the World Bank.[12]
Blanket debt cancellation would possibly result in the
escalation of civil wars. What is more, a country that has
previously proved itself unable to repay loans will find it
immensely difficult to secure another potentially vital
creditor.

Debt is not a bad thing in itself. Loans spent sensibly
have actually benefited countries. As every businessman
knows, loans are necessary to invest and expand. In the
1960s, South Korea's *per capita* income was the same as
that of Ghana's and the Ivory Coast's. Millions of formerly
destitute Bangladeshi woman have benefited from loans
from the Grameen Bank to set up businesses. Hong Kong's
post-war economy was fuelled by loans given to penniless
refugees from China.[13] Debt can boost growth, but only if
spent responsibly.

To speak in financially utilitarian terms, however, raises
further questions. Relieving Sudan's £170 million debt owed
to the British government would cost the taxpayer, as a
whole, very little. Yet, as one commentator pointed out,
£170 million would pay for a 500-bed hospital in a deprived
British city.[14] This too would save lives and relieve suffering.

The issue is more complex than many debt cancellation
supporters comprehend (although some organisations do
not call for blanket debt relief). It may be enjoyable to join
a parade or go on a train jolly to Cologne to show one's
compassion for the Third World. One may get a nice feeling
walking around with a 'Drop the Debt' T-shirt. One may

also derive a sense of righteousness by forming human chains around buildings or shoving in our faces photographs of emaciated Ethiopians. But it does not necessarily make the world a better place.

11

Relief from Celebrities

As is the norm with worthy causes, many celebrity figures emerged to support the Drop the Debt campaign. From the world of music we had Bono, Stevie Wonder, Whitney Houston, David Bowie, Luciano Pavarotti, Annie Lennox, Robbie Williams and the bands Catatonia, Oasis, The Prodigy, Cornershop and Placebo.[1] Admittedly, celebrity backing for good causes is not a very new phenomenon. Ever since The Beatles grew their hair and began holding up the two fingered peace gesture, musicians and actors have regarded it as their prerogative to promote issues of global importance. As Bono from U2 once said: 'As a pop star I have two instincts. I want to have fun. And I want to change the world'.[2] Most of the time, however, these artists do not know what they are talking about. Too often, their motive is only to help themselves.

The Scouse foursome are renowned for their subsequent solo campaigns, from John Lennon's own 1969 bed-protest for peace, to George Harrison's and Ringo Starr's benefit concert for Bangladesh in 1971, to Paul McCartney's later crusade for animal rights. In their wake came The Clash 'rocking against racism' and, most notably, the cream of British pop coming together to 'feed the world' for the Band Aid 1984 single *Do They Know It's Christmas?* and the Live Aid Wembley concert the following year. The US followed with the single *We Are the World*.

While the cult of the mass sing-in has withered, pop stars and celebrities in general still feel it part of their remit to flaunt their caring credentials, whether it be Spice Girl Geri Halliwell promoting sexual health in the Third World, supermodel Naomi Campbell telling us that wearing fur is barbaric or countless comedians and news presenters appearing bi-annually on the BBC's Comic Relief.

Former Boomtown Rats singer Bob Geldof, co-creator of Band Aid, is different from most celebrities, in that he has actually devoted much of his life to travelling in Africa with the aim of helping the starving. No one could doubt his sincerity or commitment. What is open to question is how money raised by such ventures has helped the Third World, and the sincerity of some of the celebrity campaigners involved. Live Aid raised £200 million for the 'starving of Africa'. But it did not go completely to help the needy.

During the mid-1980s, when Western money was pouring in, Ethiopia's government was embarking on a programme of Soviet-style rural collectivisation, as well as being in the midst of a prolonged civil war. Food aid did not just feed the starving, but was distributed to troops, while aid lorries were used to transport those troops. At its height, the Ethiopian defence budget accounted for 50 per cent of government expenditure and by the end of 1985, Ethiopia had the largest army in black Africa.[3] Other Band Aid proceeds, in the form of emergency shipments of yellow corn, turned up in Uganda and Tanzania, where they were seen being sold on the streets, depriving both Ethiopia's starving and hurting farmers in the latter countries by depressing the price of maize.[4] Through their display of humanity, the likes of Duran Duran, Phil Collins and Status Quo, and those who went to the record stores to purchase multiple copies of *Do They Know It's Christmas?*, unwittingly helped to prop up an incompetent and militaristic government and thus helped to send more Ethiopians to an early grave. Speaking in 2000, Rony Brauman, the former head of *Medecins Sans Frontieres*, was still bitter: 'Bob Geldof had come to Ethiopia. This concert, this nice operation with all the big people in the world meeting to express their nice feelings for the destitute and starving and the dying children and so on, this is just bullshit. I am still angry at him 15 years later, because at the time the aid was turned against the people of Ethiopia.'[5]

Celebrity naivety is often to blame here. So too is the cult of celebrity. Somehow, society deems those who we see on television to possess a firmer grasp of the world's problems.

Yet the reality is that too many entertainers simply have an infant-like compulsion to be the centre of attention: 'all actors are egomaniacs' as David Niven once remarked. They are extreme examples of our low-serotonin society in general. Too many celebrities are shallow and insecure souls who have the principal compulsion to be noticed, to be loved, and will go to all lengths to ensure this.

Often they display staggering ignorance and opportunism. For instance, in her role as UN ambassador on reproductive health, Geri Halliwell admitted to a documentary maker that she did not know the difference between 'pro-life' and 'pro-choice'. Supermodel Naomi Campbell once declared her promise never to model fur as part of a campaign for the Peta—and at a 1997 show in Milan subsequently appeared in a fur coat.[6] The singer Kim Wilde fell foul of Chris Morris in his and Armando Iannucci's 1994 BBC television satire *The Day Today*, in which she was informed of a campaign in London's West End to clamp the homeless. 'That's *terrible*', she said, doe-eyed, to the camera. U2's Bono spends his spare time lecturing government on the need to cancel Third World Debt, but thanks to the Irish Government's fiscal policy for artists, he pays barely any tax himself.[7]

The fact that Bono, real name Paul Hewson, has a fortune of more than 100 million euros but contributes so little to the welfare state of the country in which he lives appears not to trouble him. One way he could help the Third World would be to write a large cheque and send it to Oxfam, but this is not as glamorous as going on television to meet the Pope or sermonising in front of thousands at concerts. Of course, for all we know, Bono may secretly give hundreds of thousands of pounds to charity every year. If he does, that is to his credit. In July 2003, Bono threatened a campaign of civil disobedience if rich countries did not move faster to combat poverty in the Third World. 'I am ready to march with my activist friends in campaigns of civil disobedience. We are about to get very noisy, we are about to bang a lot of dustbin lids... This issue is the defining issue of our time and some of us are ready to really work on it', he said.[8]

As one of his compatriots pointed out, a traditional method of disobedience is withholding of state dues in protest of government policy.[9] Alas, this is not really a viable option for Bono, and neither is it as exciting as making loud promises.

Bono has involved himself too in BBC's *Comic Relief* campaigns, which by 1999 had raised around £140 million for worthy causes at home and abroad.[10] To its credit, *Comic Relief* has learnt from Band Aid's mistakes, sending money straight to aid agencies rather than governments. Yet it still paints a simplistic portrait of 'Africa equals good, West equals bad', and still glosses over a central matter—that starvation and poverty will only be solved in the long term if there is the absence of brutal and corrupt régimes. Perpetual aid merely allows such governments to stay in power, will never force them to address their countries' problems, and keeps sub-Saharan in the humiliating state of permanent pauperism.

Famous people who back 'uncompassionate' causes face moral censure by the care bores. In America, the pro-Republican Bo Derek claims that actors in Hollywood are denied work if they openly support the Republican party. 'They [the Democrat supporters] are very adamant and almost militant in their views' she told reporters in Hollywood in June 2000. 'It's tough to have a nice, open conversation of any kind. People get really angry and they treat me as though I'm some hateful monster.' Those who hold unfashionable opinions now keep quiet about them. High-profile Republican supporters such as Bruce Willis and Kevin Costner no longer promote their conservative views. According to one closet Republican who works for the Hollywood agency CAA: 'All the studio heads are liberals and everyone who isn't a liberal is pretending to be because they think it will help them get ahead'.[11]

The accusation that celebrities who back good causes only do so to advance their careers is not new. Neither is the rebuttal that, as Adam Smith said, self-interest can lead to the betterment of all. In keeping with the theory of the invisible hand, celebrities may be being self-centred, but if they do help to raise money, then that is for the good of all. But often their desire to appear compassionate, and the public doing likewise by going on television to hand over extremely large-sized cheques, does not actually help the poor at all.

Celebrity campaigners protest that they offer their services for free. Often this is not the case. According to an investigation by the *Sunday Telegraph* in 2003, celebrity agents often seek cash for their clients to appear backing a good cause. Posing as a bogus children's charity, *Sunday Telegraph* reporters found agents could obtain the services of 'several high-profile television presenters' for £10,000 each.[12] Even when celebrities do appear gratis, you know they will remind you of the fact at any opportunity. Like Harry Enfield's mock DJs, Smashie and Nicey, they like to tell us how they do 'a lot of work for *charidee*'.

Since the 1960s, some of the faces have gone, but some remain. In the place of the departed, we have now Robbie Williams making videos about child slavery in Africa and Coldplay and Radiohead whining about the inequities of the world. What has not changed are the same ill-informed sentiments that pour from the mouths of attention-seeking actors, singers and artists.

12

The Easiest Word

A pologising for historical wrongs is very much in vogue. Politicians, statesman and organisations are terribly eager to issue statements of repentance about the crimes of the past. Tony Blair apologised to the Irish for the potato famine, Australians have said sorry to Aborigines for colonialism, the Pope for the persecution of Galileo, the Fijians for cannibalising a British missionary in 1867, we are all contrite about the slave trade. We are all very sorry. But why?

Alongside the Nazi Holocaust, the transatlantic slave trade was one of the greatest crimes to humanity. Never was slavery practised on such a grand scale, or so brutality, and never were slave plantations created on such a level as they were by Europeans from the sixteenth to the nineteenth centuries. Today there are repeated calls from African governments to issue historical apologies. For instance, when President George W. Bush visited West Africa in July 2003, he was urged to issue contrition. Although he made references to the realities of the slave trade, he failed to apologise on behalf of the United States. This was a prudent decision. Behind the calls to ask for a simple 'sorry' lie more base motives: many African governments expect reparations to follow.

Yet, is the American government of 2003 really in a position to apologise? Are its taxpayers, who will pay for 'reparations', culpable either? The USA consists of a rainbow of races, many of whom are the descendants of the enslaved; many of whom, being post-bellum immigrants from Southern and Eastern Europe and the Far East, played no part in the slave trade; but more crucially, many of whom, black and white, are the descendants of those who fought and died to secure slavery's abolition. The West may have instigated the transatlantic slave trade, but slavery has been practised by almost all cultures. While slavery was not a distinctly Western phenomenon, the campaign to abolish it was. And the West was the first to do so.[1]

For instance, in several North American Indian tribes prior to European settlement, slaves comprised between ten and 15 per cent of the population.[2] Over centuries, black Africans participated in the trafficking and possession of slaves. In his book *The Slave Trade*, Hugh Thomas cites those groups who we should list culpable in this shameful episode in history. Alongside the Europeans, he accuses 'the rulers of Benin, the kings of Ashanti, Congo, and Dahomey, and Vili rulers of Loango, who sold great numbers of slaves over many generations'.[3] In 1807, towards the twilight of the transatlantic slave trade, there were more slaves in Africa than in the entire Americas. 'The slave trade has been the ruling principle of my people', boasted King Gezo of Dahomey in 1840. 'It is the source of their glory and wealth'.[4] It continues in Africa to this day too. It was ironic that as delegates at the 2001 World Conference Against Racism in Durban were making loud noises about reparations for slavery, that in Sudan, Mozambique and the Ivory Coast, one could still purchase slave girls for as little as £5.[5]

During Bill Clinton's tour of Africa in March 1998, in which calls for public atonement were made, President Yoweri Museveni of Uganda made an unexpected call himself. He said that chiefs of tribes who sold their own people to traders should be the ones saying sorry. 'Black traitors', he said, were more to blame than European slavers for the forcible transfer of millions of Africans to the Americas in the seventeenth and eighteenth centuries.[6] Five years later, Benin's ambassador to the US apologised to the descendants of African slaves for his country's role in this trade.[7] But this misses the point too. It was not his fault. He did not do it.

Historical apologies are about punishing the sons for the sins of the fathers, or more cynically, using the sins of one's ancestors for self-promotion, being based on a simplistic view of history. In June 1999, Tony Blair made a qualified apology to the Irish for the potato famine of the late 1840s. Why? Was it his fault? Britain did fail the Irish in the 1840s. Its attitude was certainly callous and in parts disgraceful, though ultimately it was not its fault. Ireland was reliant on a single crop and, calamitously, that crop failed.[8] Bill Clinton has apologised to the Lakota (Sioux) people of the US most famously portrayed sympathetically in Kevin Costner's *Dances With Wolves* (1990). Yet the Lakota people have not apologised to fellow Indians whose lands they stole, nor to the Pawnee tribe, whom they persecuted and carried out the tradition of murdering their warriors' wives.[9]

The Church of England was in 2000 reported to be considering issuing its own apology for the Crusades,[10] even though they happened 300 years before that Church was invented. While the Church failed to do so, its members have taken the initiative. In July 1999, 400 penitents arrived in Jerusalem for the 900th anniversary of the city's sacking by Crusaders. Calling themselves a 'pilgrimage of apology', they travelled throughout the Holy Land personally saying sorry to Arabs and Jews with the declaration: 'We deeply regret the atrocities committed in the name of Christ by our predecessors. Forgive us for allowing His name to be associated with death.'[11] Unlike pronouncing repentance for slavery, or for a 'crime' these individuals had done themselves, this gesture was absolutely meaningless. There was nothing at stake, apart from loudly proclaiming how worthy one is on a kind of sackcloth-and-ashes holiday excursion. Even those who actually know they have done nothing wrong have the desire to apologise; museum bosses around the globe have said sorry for having Nazi 'looted art' in their collections, yet sometimes that art was acquired in innocence.

The conduct of our Holy Land holidayers is reminiscent of the rock group Midnight Oil's appearance at the closing of the Sydney Olympics of 2000, in which the band sported the word 'Sorry' on their tracksuits. Midnight Oil have campaigned tiresomely for years for Aboriginal rights, and these words were in reference to the 'lost generation' of black Australians who were taken from their homes and placed with white families in the 1940s and 1950s. In that same year, white liberal Australians positively had an orgy of conspicuous compassion in this regard. In May, Sydney Harbour Bridge closed to enable 150,000 people to participate in a mass ritual of apology to Aborigines. In what the *Guardian*'s Sydney correspondent called 'a carnival atmosphere', the bridge was closed to traffic and an aeroplane wrote out the word 'sorry' high above the procession.[12] Thousands more recorded their personal apologies in special 'sorry books'. On its heels came National Reconciliation Week, with more ceremonies and speeches...

Historical apologies are arrogant and anachronistic-minded. There is the unspoken assumption that we in our supreme insight in 2004 have reached a plateau of enlightenment from which we feel able to judge all other ages. Yet it is dangerous to judge the past on the values of today. The Crusades may have been brutal, but they weren't undertaken for sheer laughs; they were undertaken by Christians who believed they were doing the right thing. Similarly, many of those behind the 'lost generation' undertook the programme in good faith, seeing it as beneficial to black Australians. In 1995 a postal campaign asked us to put our names to a petition saying sorry for the nuclear bombing of Hiroshima and Nagasaki 40 years beforehand. Yet these bombings saved the lives of thousands of Allied servicemen who were ready to invade Japan, and millions of Japanese subjects who had been instructed and were ready to fight to the death. How might today's generation feel if one day in the future Britain apologises to Germany for invading it in 1945? (With any luck, in the future we might have governments apologising for the rash of apologises issued now). Still, they abound. The Queen has apologised to the Maoris for the expropriation of their land in 1863, and the Afrikaaners for the mistreatment of Boers in British concentration camps in 1899. Bill Clinton has said sorry for medical experiments carried out on unsuspecting black Americans and John Paul II has apologised for a predecessor's treatment of Galileo.

In fact, the Pope has said sorry on nearly a hundred different occasions.[13] Yet he has not apologised for the Vatican's behaviour during the Second World War, which, if not quite as complicit as some have written, was certainly ambiguous. The Holy Father has not done so for the same reason that the Japanese have been reluctant to atone for their treatment of British PoWs during the Second World War, or that while expressing regret over Irish famine, the British government has not apologised for the 14 unarmed civilians shot dead by British soldiers in Londonderry in January 1972. The nearer the time of the historical misdemeanour, the more reluctant individuals are to express sorrow. Following the death, for instance, of Dr David Kelly over the Government's 'sexed-up' dodgy dossier on Iraq, everyone, including the BBC, expressed passive sorrow— but no one actually said sorry. When someone did try, it was couched in equivocation. Labour MP Andrew Mackinlay, who had taunted Dr Kelly during his cross-examination, said: 'I am sorry for any stress that, albeit *unintentionally*, I *may* have caused him during his questioning'. This is similar to the conditional apology issued by Cardinal Cormac Murphy-O'Connor after he was told he would not face criminal prosecution over claims he had covered up child abuse by a priest: 'I am deeply sorry for the damage that *he* has done, and to the extent that my decision contributed to any of that damage.'[14]

Sincere, unequivocal apologies for acts committed in living memory are a rare thing because, as those afflicted by such actions are still alive, the apology would actually mean something. The apologist would be forced to feel genuine regret, and pay a substantial price, whether it be emotionally or financially. A sentimentalist, said Oscar Wilde, is someone who wants the pleasure of an emotion without paying the price for it. The historical apologist is likewise out for a cheap emotional fix. Where a contemporary apology is issued, those doing so behave as if at a confessional box. By expressing contrition, the wrongdoer expects total forgiveness and to be given a clean slate. When in 2002, the Provisional IRA apologised for the killing of nearly 650 'non-combatants', it was as if it expected absolution, that this was the end of the matter. 'It's time to move on', as Martin McGuinness would say.

As the religious commentator Paul Vallely has argued, today's public, and preferably televised, form of modern confession 'misses an essential point'. He reminds us thus: 'While imprisoned in a concentration camp, Simon Wiesenthal was once confronted by a dying member of the SS seeking a Jew to confess to. "Give me absolution", the man said. But Wiesenthal would not... Only the sufferer can forgive'.[15]

13

Towards a Less 'Caring' Society

'Alas, where in the world have there been greater follies than with the compassionate? And what in the world has caused more suffering than the follies of the compassionate?'
Friedrich Nietzsche, 'Thus Spoke Zarathustra', 1883

The aim of this book is to illustrate that ostentatious 'caring' is but egotistical indulgence. Conspicuous compassion is a symptom of a fragmented society that has exchanged reason for emotion, action for gesture, cool reserve for mawkish sentimentality, individual conscience for bovine 'liberal-left' conformity. In turn, conspicuous compassion can actually harm the vulnerable—whether they be alleged paedophiles, the homeless or Africa's poor.

We want to be seen to care because we are fundamentally unhappy. In the words of that icon of conspicuous compassion, Diana, Princess of Wales, the 'biggest disease' today was 'people feeling unloved and I know that I can give love'. Diana did not have a happy life, and there is the suspicion that by wanting to be 'a Queen of people's hearts', she sought the public adoration as a way of compensation. Conspicuous compassion itself has a similar origin. We want to be seen to care because we are miserable. 'A common impulse behind wanting to give love unconditionally to nonintimates' as Oliver James concludes, 'is the desire to receive it.[1]

Isolated and divided by consumerism and lack of traditional institutions, we desperately seek a common identity and new social bonds to replace those that have withered in the post-war era—the family, the Church, the nation and neighbourhood. The bonds that arise mimic those that have withered. Recreational grieving is now our ersatz religion.

65

Following the death of celebrities, we witness rows of candles, the photograph of the 'martyr' on placards, the crowd's possession of a fierce sense of right and wrong. Mourning sickness is a religion for the lonely crowd that no longer subscribes to orthodox churches. Its flowers and teddies are its rites, its collective minutes' silences its liturgy and mass. But these new bonds are phoney, ephemeral and cynical.

It is not just immodest displays of empathy that are the problem. Less showy forms of caring, the kind you will hear articulated in the pub or at dinner parties, can be equally as self-serving and counterproductive.

For instance, it is the accepted wisdom in enlightened circles that the government should aid single parents. It is 'uncaring' or 'Victorian' to leave a single mother to her own devices. Anyone who protests to the contrary can expect to be called 'heartless' or 'a *Daily Mail* reader'. Today, nearly one in four children is raised in a single-parent family, a figure double that of the early 1980s,[2] thanks partly to punitive anti-family measures introduced under both Labour and Conservative governments.

Yet children brought up in a working-class background without the presence of fathers are much more likely to end up with poorer qualifications, lower-income jobs, unemployed, homeless or in jail.[3] Young people in lone-parent families are five times more likely to suffer physical ill-treatment than those with two birth parents, and in step-families the risk of fatal abuse is 100 times higher than in birth-parent families. Public-sanctioned, state-sponsored caring has created incalculable misery for mothers, children and society at large.

Or consider our attitude to hard drugs. It is wrong to punish hard drug users, say some. They are victims. They need support, counselling and help. The decriminalisation of serious narcotics would be better for them and society. Only since hard drugs were criminalised in the 1960s have we had a drugs problem. This is the conventional dinner party wisdom. Anyone disagreeing will be dismissed as 'draconian'. Yet most hard drug users are not simply victims: most are also dealers. They don't need help, not at least if that is methadone—a killer in its own right. In Dublin, the mortality rate from methadone is twice that of heroin itself.[4] Decriminalisation would ensnare those who are already curious. In the judgement of John Boothe Davis, head of a Scottish addiction institution: 'Most people who use drugs do so for their own reasons, on purpose, because they like it, because they find no adequate reasons for not doing so'. It is documented by many ex-heroin users that had they feared proper enforcement of anti-drug legislation, they would have never become involved in drugs in the first place.[5] We had fewer laws against hard drugs before the 1960s because there was less availability—but less demand too. Britain was a more law-abiding and cohesive place where the family, not the State, did the caring.

Then there are calls to treat prisoners with more compassion. Again, a caring attitude can be cruel. Until the 1980s, it was an offence in prison to harm yourself or to make a suicidal gesture. Unless a medic could prove that you had a legitimate illness that prompted you to act in this fashion, you were charged with wasting a doctor's time and lost remission. This regulation was abolished because it was deemed uncaring. Suicide rates in our jails have since rocketed. While the prison population of England and Wales rose from 42,000 in 1980 to 72,000 in 2002, the number of people killing themselves in our jails had quadrupled since 1983.[6]

In the wider scheme of things, compassion towards criminals has been the source of misery for law-abiding citizens. Lenient sentences are deemed more 'caring', what with crime regarded as the fault of poverty or lack of self-esteem. Yet, we would have a happier, peaceful and more just country if felons were treated 'uncaringly'. This does not mean 'getting tough', as authoritarian Home Secretaries past and present have bragged, but merely to make the punishment fit the crime. The Home Office estimates that the average offender carries out 140 offences per year. Giving Britain's small community of repeat offenders proper jail terms, as opposed to community services, would be of

enormous relief to those whose lives are blighted by crime—
that is, overwhelmingly, the poor. 'The paradox is this: the
more harshly we treat wrongdoers and the greater the
power of the state to punish them', concludes Peter
Hitchens in *A Brief History of Crime*, 'the more we preserve
liberty for the enormous majority who keep to the laws'.[7]

Elsewhere, the social worker ethic, or the compassion
compulsion, is firmly present within the National Health
Service. This means that such non-life threatening conditions as impotence, male postnatal depression, or unhappiness with one's physical appearance can be treated through
Viagra, counselling and plastic surgery—at great cost to the
NHS and to those who are actually ill with a physical
disease.

The language of caring has permeated so deeply that
even political conservatives have appropriated it. We grew
accustomed in the 1990s to Bill Clinton and Tony Blair
promising to 'reach out' to us, to 'feel' and 'care' for us.
Having won the Irish Presidency race, Mary McAleese
promised she would create 'a presidency of embrace' and of
'caring outreach' that 'holds out a hand' to victims.[8] Even
Republicans in the US and Tories in the UK now talk of
'compassionate conservatism'. The former Conservative
Chairman Theresa May thinks it bad that the Tories are
regarded as the 'nasty party'. A more helpful course of
action would be to move away from the language of 'caring'
altogether. Impersonal caring, especially at the behest of
the State, is either ineffective or counterproductive.

Politics has been corroded by this phenomenon in another
sphere. A traditional method of trying to change the world
is through the polling booth. It is no wonder turnout levels
at general elections have decreased in the last ten years.
Going to vote is a secret act through which it is impossible
to demonstrate one's virtuousness. It is far more exciting to
go on demo instead.

Likewise, helping the poor and the oppressed used to
entail going into deprived areas to help the needy. Today it
often involves merely writing a letter to a newspaper urging
for an increase in taxes. In 1994, the Bishop of Oxford

insisted that 'Taxes are a good thing and paying them is a spiritual matter'.[9] As Robert Whelan notes in *The Corrosion of Charity*:

> Instead of putting your hand in your own pocket, you can feel virtuous by demanding higher taxes to finance increased public expenditure—which is effectively putting your hand in other people's pockets.[10]

If the Good Samaritan had been raised in a culture such as ours, he would not have helped Jesus; he would have walked on by and later made a long-winded speech in the temple calling upon the Romans to tackle the 'root causes of social exclusion in Judea'. We have turned into a society of care bores. Too many today resemble Peter Simple's grotesque creation from his *Daily Telegraph* column, the sociologist Dr Heinz Kiosk, who concludes his monologues with the bellicose refrain: 'WE ARE ALL GUILTY!'

If you do genuinely care about the poor and homeless, try talking to them, or work for a charity yourself. Don't just wear an empathy ribbon: give money that might help cure life-threatening diseases. We should not be like the Pharisee, but look to the Islamic tradition of modest alms giving to deserving causes, *zakat*, one of the religion's five pillars. The Irish famine, the slave trade or the concentration camps of the past were not your fault, so stop pretending they were. Drop the slogans, give up the website petitions. If you want to stop a war, leave your ego at home. Don't feel guilty about beggars—we are not all guilty. If you need a collective buzz, don't throw eggs at paedophile suspects: start going to football games or music concerts. If you want a cathartic cry, don't misuse the death of celebrities: get out a video of *Casablanca*. Better still, turn off the television altogether. Ignore the empty promises of consumerism. Get to know your neighbours, talk to your friends and family a bit more. Most of all, next time you profess that you 'care' about something, consider your motives and the consequences of your words and actions. Sometimes, the only person you really care about is you.

Postscript

The Case of the Rev. John Smallwood

2003 saw the 40th anniversary of the film *Heavens Above!* It stars Peter Sellers as the Rev. John Smallwood, an idealistic and cheerful prison chaplain who is appointed vicar of Orbiston Parva by mistake. He gives shelter to a workshy, benefits-rich tribe with their many offspring. He befriends Lady Despard, widow of the founder of the local chemical firm Tranquilax, which is the town's main employer. Through her financial generosity, they embark on a programme of helping the needy by giving away food and provisions. Having gained national fame through his programme of philanthropy, he goes on to denounce Tranquilax from the pulpit. The results are catastrophic. Tranquilax stocks are sent crashing and its workers are laid off. Mr Smallwood's caring programme puts custom-starved local butchers, bakers and supermarkets out of business. Local unemployment tops 60 per cent.

Everyone opposed to Mr Smallwood's kind gestures is portrayed as money-grabbing, selfish, hypocritical and small-minded. Smallwood is unpretentious and resilient and he and his companion, a black dustman, are the only sympathetic characters in the movie. The film tells us that when it comes to impersonal caring, society is divided into two camps: the romantic but wrong and the revolting but right.

Notes

1: Conspicuous Compassion

1   The *Spectator*, 3 May 2003.

2   See Mesotrovic, S.G., *Postemotional Society*, London: Sage Publications, 1996.

3   *Daily Mail*, 20 June 2002.

4   Cashmore, E., ...*And There Was Television*, London: Routledge, 1994.

5   The number of prescriptions for all types of anti-depressants in England rose from 10.8 million in 1993 to 26.6 million in 2002. (*The Times*, 20 October 2003.)

6   James, O., *Britain on the Couch, Why We're Unhappier Compared with 1950 Despite Being Richer*, London: Arrow Books, 1998, p. 21, p.157.

7   *Sunday Times*, 17 July 2003.

8   James, *Britain on the Couch*, 1998, p. 20, p. 184.

9   James, *Britain on the Couch*, 1998, p. 132.

10 Veblen, T., *The Theory of the Leisure Class, An Economic Study of Institutions* (1912), London: George Allen & Unwin, 1924, pp. 72, 74.

2: Mourning Sickness

1   Cited by Mick Hume, *LM*, October 1997.

2   Both cited by Furedi, F., *Culture of Fear, Risk-Taking and the Morality of Low Expectation*, London: Cassell, 1997, p. 174.

3   O'Hear, A., in Anderson, D. and Mullen, P. (eds), *Faking It: The Sentimentalisation of Modern Society*, London: Social Affairs Unit, 1998, p. 184.

4   O'Hear, *Faking It*, 1998, p. 184.

5   *Daily Telegraph*, 17 April 1998.

6   Interviews by Brendan O'Neill, *LM*, October 1997.

7   *Granta*, 60, Winter 1997, p. 30, pp. 10-17 *passim*.

8   *Daily Mirror*, 27 April 1999.

9   *Sun*, 10 August 1999.

10 *Sunday Mirror*, 25 August 2002; *Sunday Express*, 25 August 2002.

11 *Sunday Telegraph*, 23 June 2003.

12 *Daily Telegraph*, 13 September 2002.

13 *Sunday Times*, 3 August 2003.

3: Nonce-sense

1   *Daily Telegraph*, 17 December 2001.

2   *Sunday Telegraph*, 3 September 2000.

3   *Observer*, 25 August 2002.

4   *Sunday Telegraph*, 23 February 1997; *Guardian*, 24 July 2000.

5   Furedi, F., *Paranoid Parenting, Abandon Your Anxieties and be a Good Parent*, London: Allen Lane, 2001, p. 15.

6   *Herald*, 21 December 2002; *Daily Telegraph*, 15 January 2003.

7   *The Times*, 28 July 2003.

8   *Daily Telegraph*, 9 February 2001.

9   Furedi, *Paranoid Parenting*, 2001, pp. 10-11.

10 *Daily Mail*, 28 July 2001.

4: Silence of the Critics

1   Howard, P., *The Times*, 15 September 2001.

2   *Sun*, 29 September 2002.

3   *Western Morning News*, 11 October 1999.

4   *Guardian*, 4 October 1993.

5   *Journal* (Newcastle), 10 February 2001.

6   Cited by Hume, M., *The Times*, 14 September 2002.

7   *The Times*, 14 September 2002.

8   www.rivals.net

9   *The Times*, 22 November 1938; 10 May 1953.

5: Lapel Louts

1   See a guide to ribbons, logged 15 July 2003,
    goldnthings.com/awareness_ribbons.htm

2   *The Times*, 3 September 1997; Jasper Pleydell-
    Bouverie, *Independent*, 1 December 1997.

3   The *Spectator*, 13 December 2003.

4   *The Times*, 14 July 2003; *Times Higher Educational
    Supplement*, 12 June 1996.

5   *News of The World*, 20 April 2003. Emphasis in
    original.

6   *Daily Express*, 24 October 2002.

7   One study has found that as little as two per cent of the
    price of each box of charity cards sold in large high
    street stores ends up going to good causes, with most of
    the money being pocketed by manufacturers, retailers
    and the taxman. (*Sunday Telegraph*, 30 November
    2003.)

8   BBC news website 5 March 1999, logged 24 September
    2003, www.cafonline.org

9   *The Times*, 20 August 2003.

6: Animal Wrongs

1   *Guardian*, 27 December 2002.

2   Cited in the *Independent*, 5 April 2002.

3   *Daily Telegraph*, 9 July 2003.

4   DeGrazia, David, *Animal Rights, A Very Short
    Introduction*, Oxford University Press, 2002, p. 71.

5   Vegetarian Society, logged 13 July 2003,
    www.vegsoc.org

6   *Prospect*, May 2001.

7   DeGrazia, *Animal Rights*, 2002, pp. 67-80; Vegetarian
    Society, logged on 13 July 2003, www.vegsoc.org

8   *The Times*, 12 July 2003.

9   Aitkenhead, D., *Observer*, 17 August 2003.

10 Tester, K., *Animals and Society: The Humanity of Animal Rights*, London: Routledge, 1991.

7: Any Spare Change

1 *Independent*, 1 November 1997.

2 *Independent*, 15 March 2000.

3 *Independent*, 2 November 2000.

4 *Independent on Sunday*, 24 December 2000.

5 *Observer*, 14 July 2002.

6 *Guardian*, 10 October 2000, 22 August 2003.

7 *Sunday Times*, 1 October 2000.

8 *Daily Star*, 21 May 2003.

9 *Sunday Times*, 1 October 2000.

10 *Guardian*, 10 October 2000.

11 *Daily Star*, 21 May 2003.

12 *Guardian*, 23 July 2003.

13 Bird, J., *Retreat From the Streets*, London: Politeia, 2002, p. 8.

14 Dennis, N. and Erdos, G., *Families Without Fatherhood* (third edition), London: Civitas, 2000.

15 Bird, *Retreat From the Streets*, 2002, p. 9.

16 Dean, H., *Begging Questions: Street-level Economic Activity and Social Policy Failure*, 1999, in the *Guardian*, 15 September 1999.

17 Humphreys, R., *No Fixed Abode: A History of Responses to the Roofless and the Rootless in Britain*, London: Macmillan, 1999, p. 158.

8: Not in My Name

1 Ali, T. and Watkins, S., *1968, Marching in the Streets*, London: Bloomsbury, 1998, p. 7.

2 *Sunday Herald* (Glasgow), 16 February 2003.

3 Spiked-online.com, 1 November 2002.

4 *Guardian*, 29 March 2003.

5 *Mail on Sunday*, 16 February 2003.

6 *Guardian*, 6 February 2003.

7 www.seattlewto.org/n30/call/eng.html, logged 3 December 1999.

8 Monbiot, G., *The Age of Consent, A Manifesto For A New World Order*, London: Flamingo, 2003.

9 Monbiot, *The Age of Consent*, 2003, p. 2.

10 *The Times*, 2 December 1999.

11 *Sunday Herald* (Glasgow), 16 February 2003.

12 *Guardian*, 25 September 1982.

9: You've Got Junk Mail

1 *Guardian*, 6 May 2003.

2 www.thepetitionsite.com, logged 18 July 2003.

3 commemoratewtc.com, logged 22 July 2003.

4 www.nealcomm.com/condolences

5 www.livejournal.com/users/luckyme/251991.html, logged on 18 July 2003.

6 www.wired.com, 22 April 2003 by Christopher Null.

10: Drop the Slogans

1 *The Times*, 18 June 1999.

2 *The Times*, 18 June 1999.

3 *Sunday Telegraph*, 21 February 1999.

4 *The Times*, 27 April 1999.

5 *Independent*, 20 June 1999.

6 *The Times*, 19 November 1998.

7 Camilla Cavendish, *The Times*, 29 May 2003.

8 Vallely, P., *Bad Samaritans, First World Ethics and Third World Debt*, London: Hodder & Stoughton, 1990, p. 153.

9 Vallely, *Bad Samaritans,* 1990, p. 157.

10 Vallely, *Bad Samaritans,* 1990, p. 158.

11 *The Times*, 19 November 1998.

12 *Sunday Telegraph*, 21 February 1999.

13 *The Times*, 27 April 1999.

14 Martin Vander Weyer, *Sunday Telegraph*, 21 February 1999.

11: Relief from Celebrities

1   *Independent*, 11 February 1999.

2   *Guardian*, 16 February 1999.

3   Vallely, P., *Bad Samaritans, First World Ethics and Third World Debt*, London: Hodder & Stoughton, 1990, p. 153.

4   *Guardian*, 28 May 2003; *The Times*, 29 May 2003.

5   *The Times*, 9 November 2000.

6   *Guardian*, 3 August 2001.

7   *Sunday Telegraph*, 23 June 2003.

8   *Irish Independent*, 9 July 2003.

9   Liam Fay, *Sunday Times* (Dublin edition), 27 July 2003.

10 *Daily Mail*, 8 March 1999.

11 *Daily Telegraph*, 9 June 2000.

12 *Sunday Telegraph*, 15 June 2003.

12: The Easiest Word

1   See D'Souza, D., *The End of Racism, Principles for a Multiracial Society*, New York: The Free Press, 1995, p. 100 and pp. 67-144, *passim*.

2   D'Souza, *The End of Racism,* 1995, p. 73.

3   Thomas, H., *The Slave Trade, The History of the Atlantic Slave Trade: 1440-1870*, London: Picador, 1997, p. 13.

4   Thomas, *The Slave Trade,* 1997, p. 559 & p. 673.

5   *Sunday Telegraph*, 9 September 2001.

6   *Guardian*, 23 March 1998.

7 *Observer*, 6 July 2003.

8 See Toibin, C. and Ferriter, D., *The Irish Famine, a documentary*, London: Profile, 1999.

9 *Times Literary Supplement*, 15 August 2003.

10 *Daily Mail*, 14 March 2000.

11 *Independent on Sunday*, 18 July 1999.

12 *Guardian*, 29 May 2000.

13 *Times Literary Supplement*, 1 August 2003.

14 *Evening Standard* (London), 22 July 2003, emphasis added.

15 *Independent*, 26 November 1997.

13: Towards a Less 'Caring' Society

1 James, O., *Britain on the Couch, Why We're Unhappier Compared with 1950 Despite Being Richer*, London: Arrow Books, 1998, p. 77.

2 *Daily Mail*, 8 May 2003.

3 Dennis, N. and Erdos, G., *Families Without Fatherhood* (third edition), London: Civitas, 2000.

4 Kenny, M., *Death by Heroin, Recovery by Hope*, Dublin: New Island Books, 1999, p. 140.

5 Kenny, *Death by Heroin*, 1999, p. 117.

6 Hitchens, P., *A Brief History of Crime, The Decline of Order, Justice and Liberty in England*, London: Atlantic Books, 2003, pp. 133, 145.

7 Hitchens, *A Brief History of Crime*, 2003, p. 8.

8 Cited by Frank Furedi, *LM*, March 1998.

9 *The Times*, 15 October 1994.

10 Whelan, R., *The Corrosion of Charity, From Moral Renewal to Contract Culture*, London: IEA Health and Welfare Unit, 1996, p. 82.